RUSSIAN

in 10 minutes a day

by **Kristine Kershul**, M.A., University of California, Santa Barbara

adapted by **Helen Adelbera McIntyre**, Ed.D.

Published by

Bilingual Books, Inc.
511 Eastlake Ave. E.
Seattle, Washington   98109, U.S.A.
(206) 624-5344

Distributed by
USA: Cliffs Notes, Inc., Box 80728, Lincoln, Nebraska 68501
Canada: Beaverbooks, 195 Allstate Parkway, Markham, Ontario L3R 4T8
UK: Bilingual Books, 8 Wardlaw Terrace, Edinburgh 11, Scotland

(ahl-fah-veet)
Алфавит
alphabet

When you first see words like „машина" and „когда", Russian can appear to be forbidding. However, it is not, when you know how to decode these new letters. To learn these new Russian letters, work through the examples here and on pages 106 and 107. Above all new words is a very easy pronunciation guide. These pages are intended as a guide, so mark them and refer to them whenever you need help. The entire Russian alphabet can be found on page 107.

There are five letters that look and sound like English:

(ah)	*(k)*	*(m)*	*(oh)*	*(t)*
А	**К**	**М**	**О**	**Т**

You can already say:

(kahk)
как *как, как, как, как*
how

(koht)
кот _____
cat

(ktoh)
кто _____
who

(tahm)
там _____
there

Russian has seven letters that look like English, but be careful; they are not pronounced like English.

(v)	*(eh/yeh)*	*(n)*	*(r)*	*(s)*	*(oo)*	*(h)*
В	**Е**	**Н**	**Р**	**С**	**У**	**Х**

Now pronounce these words:

(voht)
вот _____
here

(stoh)
сто _____
100

(mar-kah)
марка _____
stamp

(sah-har)
сахар _____
sugar

(ahn-tyen-nah)
антенна _____
antenna

(soh-oos)
соус _____
sauce

(kahs-sah)
касса _____
cashier

(kar-tah)
карта _____
map

(too-mahn)
туман _____
foggy

(hah-ohs)
хаос _____
chaos

These Russian letters look quite different from English. With only a couple of exceptions, they are easy to pronounce once you learn them. Are you ready? First practice writing these new letters.

(b)	*(g)*	*(d)*	*(yoh)*	*(zh)*	*(z)*
б *б, б*	**г** ___	**д** ___	**ё** ___	**ж** ___	**з** ___
(ee)	*(l)*	*(p)*	*(f)*	*(ts)*	*(ch)*
и ___	**л** ___	**п** ___	**ф** ___	**ц** ___	**ч** ___
(sh)	*(shch/sht)*	*(eh)*	*(yoo)*	*(yah)*	
ш ___	**щ** ___	**э** ___	**ю** ___	**я** ___	

Now let's try a few simple words:

(bahnk)
банк *банк*
bank

(kahg-dah)
когда _____
when

(kahv-yor)
ковёр _____
carpet

(zhah-kyet)
жакет _____
jacket

(zoh-nah)
зона _____
zone

(tahk-see)
такси _____
taxi

Seven Key Question Words

When you arrive in the *(sah-vyet-skee)* *(sah-yooz)* **Советский Союз,** the very first thing you will need to do is ask
Soviet Union

questions—"Where is the bus stop?" "Where can I exchange money?" "Where *(gdyeh)* **(где)** is the

lavatory?" "*(gdyeh)* **Где** is a restaurant?" "*(gdyeh)* **Где** do I catch a taxi?" "*(gdyeh)* **Где** is a good hotel?"
where where where

"*(gdyeh)* **Где** is my luggage?"—and the list will go on and on for the entire length of your visit.

In Russian, there are SEVEN KEY QUESTION WORDS to learn. For example, the seven

key question words will help you find out exactly what you are ordering in a restaurant

before you order it—and not after the surprise (or shock!) arrives. Notice that "what"

and "who" are differentiated by only one letter, so be sure not to confuse them.

Take a few minutes to study and practice saying the seven basic question words listed

below. Then cover the *(roos-skee)* **русский** with your hand and fill in each of the blanks with the
Russian

matching *(roos-skee-mee)* *(slah-vah-mee)* **русскими словами.**
Russian word

1.	*(gdyeh)* **ГДЕ**	=	WHERE	где, где, где, где, где
2.	*(chtoh)* **ЧТО**	=	WHAT	_____
3.	*(ktoh)* **КТО**	=	WHO	_____
4.	*(kahk)* **КАК**	=	HOW	_____
5.	*(kahg-dah)* **КОГДА**	=	WHEN	_____
6.	*(pah-chee-moo)* **ПОЧЕМУ**	=	WHY	_____
7.	*(skohl-kah)* **СКОЛЬКО**	=	HOW MUCH	_____

Now test yourself to see if you really can keep these *(slah-vah)* **слова** straight in your mind. Draw
words

lines between the *(roos-skee-mee) (ee)* **русскими и** English equivalents below.
Russian   and

why   *(kahg-dah)* **когда**

what   *(skohl-kah)* **сколько**

who   *(pah-chee-moo)* **почему**

how   *(gdyeh)* **где**

where   *(ktoh)* **кто**

when   *(chtoh)* **что**

how much   *(kahk)* **как**

Examine the following questions containing these words. Practice the sentences out loud *(ee)* **и**
and

then quiz yourself by filling in the blanks below with the correct question *(slah-vah-mee)* **словами.**
word

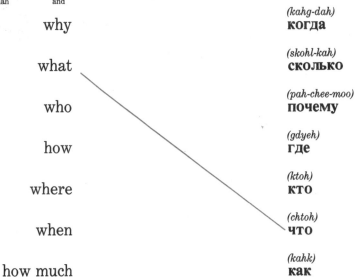

(gdyeh) (sah-laht)
Где салат?
where is   the salad

(ktoh) (et-tah)
Кто это?
who is   that?

(kahg-dah) (bahl-yet)
Когда балет?
when is   the ballet

(chtoh) (et-tah)
Что это?
what is   that?

(kahk) (dee-lah)
Как дела?
how are things/how are you

(skohl-kah) (et-tah)(stoy-eet)
Сколько это стоит?
how much does   that   cost

1. _____ *(dee-lah)* **дела?**

2. _____ *(et-tah) (stoy-eet)* **это стоит?**
that   cost

3. _____ Кто _____ *(et-tah)* **это?**
that

4. _____ *(et-tah)* **это?**
that

5. _____ *(bahl-yet)* **балет?**
ballet

6. _____ *(sah-laht)* **салат?**
salad

(gdyeh)
„**Где**" will be your most used question *(sloh-vah)* **слово,** so let's concentrate on it. Say each of the
where   *word*

(roos-skah-yeh)
following **русское** sentences aloud. Then write out each sentence without looking at the
Russian

example. If you don't succeed on the first try, don't give up. Just practice each sentence

until you are able to do it easily. Remember „**c**" is pronounced like an "s" *(ee)* **и** „**p**" is

4 pronounced like an "r."

(gdyeh) *(too-ahl-yet)*
Где туалет?
where is a toilet

(gdyeh) *(tahk-see)*
Где такси?
where is a taxi

(gdyeh) *(ahv-toh-boos)*
Где автобус?
where is a bus

Где такси?

(res-tah-rahn)
Где ресторан?
a restaurant

(bahnk)
Где банк?
a bank

(ah-tyel)
Где { **отель?**
a hotel
(gah-stee-neet-sah)
гостиница?
a hotel/an inn

(dah)
Да, you can see similarities between **русским и английским,** if you look closely.
yes   *(roos-skeem)* *(ee)* *(ahn-glee-skeem)*
Russian   and English

(roos-skee) *(ee)* *(ahn-glee-skee)*
Русский и английский are not related languages, but some words are surprisingly
and

similar. Of course, they do not always sound the same when spoken by a Russian, but the

similarities will certainly surprise you and make your work here easier. Listed below are

(slohv)   *(ah)*   *(sloh-vah)*
five "free" **слов** beginning with „**а**" to help you get started. Be sure to say each **слово**
words

(ee)   *(roos-skah-yeh)* *(sloh-vah)*
aloud **и** then write out the **русское слово** in the blank to the right.
Russian   word

☑ **абрикос** *(ah-bree-kohs)* . . . . apricot   _____
☑ **август** *(ahv-goost)* . . . . August   _____
☑ **авиация** *(ah-vee-aht-see-yah)* . . . . aviation   **а**   _____
☑ **Австралия** *(ahv-strah-lee-yah)* . . . . Australia   _____
☑ **Австрия** *(ahv-stree-yah)* . . . . Austria   _____

(sloh-vah)
Free **слова** like these will appear at the bottom of the following pages in a yellow color
words

band. They are easy—enjoy them! Don't forget to pronounce „**и**" as "ee."

5

Step 2 — Odds 'n Ends

(roos-skee) *(yah-zik)* **Русский язык** does not have *(slohv)* **слов** for "the" and "a," which makes things easier for you.
Russian language words

Russian *(sloh-vah)* **слова** also change their endings depending on how they are used, so don't be
words

surprised! Learn *(sloh-vah)* **слова** and be prepared to see their endings change. Here are some
the words

examples.

(sloh-vah) **СЛОВО** word	*(kuh-nee-gah)* **КНИГА** book	*(stool)* **СТУЛ** chair
(slah-vah) **СЛОВА**	*(kuh-nee-gee)* **КНИГИ**	*(stool-ah)* **СТУЛА**
(sloh-voo) **СЛОВУ**	*(kuh-nee-geh)* **КНИГЕ**	*(stool-oo)* **СТУЛУ**
(sloh-vahm) **СЛОВОМ**	*(kuh-nee-goo)* **КНИГУ**	*(stool-ohm)* **СТУЛОМ**
(slohv) **СЛОВ**	*(kuh-nee-goy)* **КНИГОЙ**	*(stool-yeh)* **СТУЛЕ**
(sloh-vah-mee) **СЛОВАМИ**	*(kuh-neeg)* **КНИГ**	*(stool-yah)* **СТУЛЬЯ**

This only appears difficult because it is different from *(ahn-glee-skoh-vah)* *(yah-zih-kah)* **английского языка.** Just remember
English language

the core of *(sloh-vah)* **слова** doesn't change, so you'll always be able to recognize it. For instance,
the word

you will be understood whether you say *(kuh-nee-gah)* **книга** or *(kuh-nee-goo)* **книгу.** Learn to look for the core of the
book

word, and don't worry about the different endings.

Step 3 — Look Around You

Before you proceed *(suh)* **с** this Step, situate yourself comfortably in your living room.
with

Now look around you. Can you name the things that you see in this *(kohm-naht-yeh)* **комнате** in Russian?
room

You can probably guess *(lahm-pah)* **лампа** and maybe even *(dee-vahn)* **диван.** But let's learn the rest of them.
lamp divan/couch

After practicing these *(slah-vah)* **слова** out loud, write them in the blanks below *(ee)* **и** on the next page.
words and

(kar-tee-nah) *(kar-teen-kah)* **картина/картинка** picture _____

(pah-tah-lohk) **ПОТОЛОК** = ceiling ПОТОЛОК , ПОТОЛОК , ПОТОЛОК

☐ **автобиография** *(ahv-toh-bee-oh-grah-fee-yah)*. autobiography _____
☐ **автограф** *(ahv-toh-grahf)*............... autograph _____
☐ **автомат** *(ahv-toh-maht)*.............. automat **а** _____
☐ **автомобиль** *(ahv-tah-mah-beel)*........... automobile _____
☐ **автор** *(ahv-tar)*...................... author _____

(oog-ahl) **угол**	=	corner	_____
(ahk-noh) **окно**	=	window	_____
(lahm-pah) **лампа**	=	lamp, light	*лампа, лампа, лампа*
(dee-vahn) **диван**	=	sofa	_____
(stool) **стул**	=	chair	_____
(kahv-yor) **ковёр**	=	carpet	_____
(stohl) **стол**	=	table	_____
(dvyair) **дверь**	=	door	_____
(chah-see) **часы**	=	clock	_____
(zah-nahv-yes) **занавес**	=	curtain	_____
(styen-ah) **стена**	=	wall	_____
(teh-leh-fohn) **телефон**	=	telephone	_____

In Step 2, you learned that **русские** *(roos-skee-yeh)* **слова** *(slah-vah)* vary. The correct form of each **слово** *(sloh-vah)* will
Russian   words   word

always be given to familiarize you with the variations. Now open your **книгу** *(kuh-nee-goo)* to the
book

sticky labels (between pages 48 and 49). Peel off the first 14 labels **и** *(ee)* proceed around the
and

комнаты *(kohm-nah-tee)* labeling these items in your home. This will help to increase your **русское** *(roos-skah-yeh)*
room   Russian

слово *(sloh-vah)* power easily. Don't forget to say each **слово** *(sloh-vah)* as you attach each label.
word   word

Now ask yourself, ,,**Где** *(gdyeh)* **картина?**" *(kar-tee-nah)* and point at it while you answer, ,,**Там картина.**" *(tahm) (kar-tee-nah)*
the picture   there is the picture

Continue on down the list until you feel comfortable with these new **словами.** *(slah-vah-mee)* Say,
words

,,**Где** *(gdyeh)* **потолок?**" *(pah-tah-lohk)* Then reply, ,,**Там** *(tahm)* **потолок,**" *(pah-tah-lohk)* and so on. When you can identify all the
the ceiling   there is

items on the list, you will be ready to move on. Now, starting on the next page, let's learn

some basic parts of the house.

☐ **агент** *(ah-gyent)*......................	agent
☐ **адвокат** *(ahd-vah-kaht)*..................	advocate, lawyer
☐ **адрес** *(ah-dres)*......................	address
☐ **Азия** *(ah-zee-yah)*......................	Asia
☐ **академия** *(ah-kah-dyeh-mee-yah)*..........	academy

a

7

(dohm)
дом = house

(voht) *(dohm)*
Вот дом.
here is   the house

(kah-bee-nyet)
кабинет
study

(vahn-nah-yah)
ванная
bathroom

(koohk-nyah)
кухня
kitchen

(spahl-nyah)
спальня
bedroom

(stah-loh-vah-yah)
столовая
dining room

(gah-stee-nah-yah)
гостиная
living room

(gah-rahzh)
гараж
garage

(pahd-vahl)
подвал
basement

While learning these new *(slah-vah)* **слова,** let's not forget
words

(ahv-tah-mah-beel) *(mah-shee-nah)*
автомобиль/машина
automobile/car

(moh-tah-tsee-kul)
мотоцикл
motorcycle

(sah-bah-kah)
собака
dog

МОТОЦИКЛ

☐ **аккуратный** *(ahk-koo-raht-nee)*	fastidious, neat
☐ **акробат** *(ah-krah-baht)*	acrobat
☐ **акт** *(ahkt)*	act
☐ **актёр** *(ahk-tyor)*	actor
☐ **акцент** *(ahkt-syent)*	accent

а

8

(koht)
КОТ
cat

(sahd)
сад
garden

(poach-tah)
почта
mail

КОТ, КОТ, КОТ _____ _____

(putch-toh-vee) *(yahsh-chik)*
ПОЧТОВЫЙ ЯЩИК
mailbox

(tsvet-ee)
цветы
flowers

(zvah-nohk)
ЗВОНОК
doorbell

_____ _____ _____

Peel off the next set of labels *(ee)* **и** wander through your **дом** *(dohm)* learning these new **слова.** *(slah-vah)*
words

Granted, it will be somewhat difficult to label your **кот,** *(koht)* **цветы** *(tsvet-ee)* or **собаку,** *(sah-bah-koo)* but use your
cat flowers dog
imagination. Again, practice by asking yourself, „**Где** *(gdyeh)* **автомобиль?**" *(ahv-tah-mah-beel)* and reply,
the car

„**Вот автомобиль.**" *(voht) (ahv-tah-mah-beel)*
here is

Now for the following... **Где собака? Где...**

Step 4

(ah-deen) **Один,** one	*(dvah)* **два,** two	*(tree)* **три** three			

один   два   три   четыре   пять   шесть

Consider for a minute how important numbers are. How could you tell someone your phone number, your address *(ee-lee)* **или** your hotel room if you had no numbers? And think of or how difficult it would be if you could not understand the time, the price of an apple *(ee-lee)* **или** the or correct bus to take. When practicing the *(chee-slah)* **числа** below, notice the similarities (underlined) numbers between *(ah-deen)* **один** and *(ah-deen-nud-tset)* **одиннадцать,** *(tree)* **три** and *(tree-nod-tset)* **тринадцать,** and so on.
one   eleven   three   thirteen

0	*(nohl)* **ноль**			0	ноль, ноль, ноль, ноль
1	*(ah-deen)* **один**	11	*(ah-deen-nud-tset)* **одиннадцать**	1	_____
2	*(dvah)/(dveh)* **два/две**	12	*(dveh-nod-tset)* **двенадцать**	2	_____
3	*(tree)* **три**	13	*(tree-nod-tset)* **тринадцать**	3	_____
4	*(cheh-tir-ee)* **четыре**	14	*(cheh-tir-nod-tset)* **четырнадцать**	4	_____
5	*(pyaht)* **пять**	15	*(pyaht-nod-tset)* **пятнадцать**	5	_____
6	*(shest)* **шесть**	16	*(shest-nod-tset)* **шестнадцать**	6	_____
7	*(syem)* **семь**	17	*(sim-nod-tset)* **семнадцать**	7	_____
8	*(voh-syem)* **восемь**	18	*(vah-sim-nod-tset)* **восемнадцать**	8	_____
9	*(dyev-yet)* **девять**	19	*(div-yet-nod-tset)* **девятнадцать**	9	_____
10	*(dyes-yet)* **десять**	20	*(dvahd-tset)* **двадцать**	10	_____

☐ **алло!** *(ahl-loh)* . . . . hello!
☐ **Англия** *(ahn-glee-yah)* . . . . England
☐ —where they speak **по-английски** *(pah-ahn-glee-skee)*
☐ —**англичанин** *(ahn-glee-chahn-een)* . . . . Englishman
☐ —**англичанка** *(ahn-glee-chahn-kah)* . . . . Englishwoman

a

_____
_____
_____
_____

10

Use these **числа** *(chee-slah)* on a daily basis. Count to yourself **по-русски** *(pah-roos-skee)* when you brush your teeth,
numbers   in   Russian

exercise, **или** *(ee-lee)* commute to work. Now fill in the following blanks according to the **числам** *(chee-slahm)*
or   numbers

given in parentheses.

Note: This is a good time to start learning these two **очень** *(oh-cheen)* important phrases.
very

(yah)	*(hah-choo)*	*(koo-peet)*			
Я	**хочу**	**купить**	=	I would like to buy	_____
(mwee)	*(hah-teem)*	*(koo-peet)*			
МЫ	**ХОТИМ**	**КУПИТЬ**	=	we would like to buy	_____

(yah) **Я** I	*(hah-choo)* **хочу** would like	*(koo-peet)* **купить** to buy	*(et-tah)* **это.** that		*(skohl-kah)* **Сколько?** how many	_____ (2)
(yah) **Я** I	*(hah-choo)* **хочу** would like	*(koo-peet)* **купить** to buy	_____ (1) .		*(skohl-kah)* **Сколько?** how many	_____ (1)
Я I	*(hah-choo)* **хочу** would like	*(koo-peet)* **купить**	_____ (7)	*(mar-ahk)* **марок.** stamps	*(skohl-kah)* **Сколько?** how many	_____ (7)
Я	*(hah-choo)* **хочу**	*(koo-peet)* **купить**	_____ (8)	*(mar-ahk)* **марок.** stamps	*(skohl-kah)* **Сколько?**	_____ (8)
Я	*(hah-choo)* **хочу**	*(koo-peet)* **купить**	*ПЯТЬ* (5) .		*(skohl-kah)* **Сколько?**	_____ (5)
(mwee) **Мы** we	*(hah-teem)* **хотим** would like	*(koo-peet)* **купить** to buy	_____ (9)	*(aht-krit-tahk)* **открыток.** postcards	*(skohl-kah)* **Сколько?**	_____ (9)
(mwee) **Мы** we	*(hah-teem)* **хотим** would like	**купить**	_____ (10)	*(aht-krit-tahk)* **открыток.** postcards	*(skohl-kah)* **Сколько?**	_____ (10)
(mwee) **Мы** we	*(hah-teem)* **хотим** would like	**купить**	_____ (6) .	ПАРТЕР	*(skohl-kah)* **Сколько?**	*шесть* (6)
(yah) **Я** I	*(hah-choo)* **хочу** would like	**купить**	_____ (1)	*(beel-yet-tee)* **билеты.** ticket	*(skohl-kah)* **Сколько?**	_____ (1)
(mwee) **Мы** we	*(hah-teem)* **хотим** would like	**купить**	_____ (4)	*(beel-yet-tah)* **билета.** tickets	*(skohl-kah)* **Сколько?**	_____ (4)
	(hah-teem) **Мы хотим** would like	**купить**	_____ (11) .		**Сколько?**	_____ (11)
(yah) **Я** 	*(hah-choo)* **хочу** would like	**купить**	_____ (3)	*(chahsh-kee)* **чашки** *(chah-yah)* **чая.** cups of tea	**Сколько?**	_____ (3)
	(hah-teem) **Мы хотим** would like	**купить** to buy	_____ (4)	*(chahsh-kee)* **чашки** *(kohf-yeh)* **кофе.** cups of coffee	**Сколько?**	_____ (4)

☐ **анекдот** *(ah-nek-doht)*	anecdote, joke		_____
☐ **антенна** *(ahn-tyen-nah)*	antenna		_____
☐ **антибиотики** *(ahn-tee-bee-oh-tee-kee)*	antibiotics	**а**	_____
☐ **аппетит** *(ahp-peh-teet)*	appetite		_____
☐ **апрель** *(ahp-ryel)*	April		_____

Now see if you can translate the following thoughts **на** **русский.** *(nah)* *(roos-skee)* into Russian **Ответы** are at the *(aht-vyet-ee)* the answers bottom of the page.

1. I would like to buy seven postcards.

_____

2. I would like to buy nine stamps. _____

3. We would like to buy four cups of tea.

Мы хотим купить четыре чашки чая.

4. We would like to buy three tickets.

_____

Review **числа** 1 through 20 **и** answer the following **вопросы** aloud, **и** then write the *(chee-slah)* numbers *(ee)* and *(vah-proh-see)* questions *(ee)* answers in the blank spaces.

(skohl-kah) *(zdyes)* *(stah-lohv)*
Сколько **здесь** **столов?**
how many · here · tables

три

(skohl-kah) *(zdyes)* *(lahmp)*
Сколько **здесь** **ламп?**
here · lamps

_____

(skohl-kah) *(zdyes)* *(stool-yehv)*
Сколько **здесь** **стульев?**
chairs

_____

12

(skohl-kah) **(zdyes)** **(chah-sohv)**
Сколько здесь часов?
how many · here · clocks

_____

(skohl-kah) **(zdyes)** **(oh-kahn)**
Сколько здесь окон?
windows

_____

(skohl-kah) **(zdyes)** **(dyet-yeh)**
Сколько здесь детей?
children

три

(skohl-kah) **(zdyes)** **(kuh-neeg)**
Сколько здесь книг?
books

_____

(skohl-kah) **(zdyes)** **(lood-yeh)**
Сколько здесь людей
people

_____

(tsvet-ah)
Цвета
colors

Step 5

(tsvet-ah) **(pah-roos-skee)** **(pah-ahn-glee-skee)** **(ee-men-ah)**
Цвета are the same **по-русски** as they are **по-английски**—they just have different **имена.**
colors · in Russian · in English · names

(tsvet) **(sah-vyet-skahm)** **(sah-yoo-zeh)**
Red is the national **цвет** in **Советском Союзе.** You will see it everywhere you go—on the
color · the Soviet · Union

(krahs-nee) **(ee)** **(zhyol-tee)** **(ee)** **(tsvet-ah)**
flag, which is **красный и жёлтый,** in clothing **и** on banners. Let's learn the basic **цвета.**
red · and yellow · colors

(strah-neet-seh) **(roos-skee-yeh)**
Once you have read through the list on the next **странице,** cover the **русские** with your
page · Russian

(ee) **(roos-skah-yeh)**
hand, **и** practice writing out **русское** next to the English.
the Russian

(tsvet-ah)
Once you've learned **цвета,** quiz yourself. What color are your shoes? Your eyes?
the colors

Your hair?

☐ **арена** _(ar-yen-ah)_ . . . . arena _____
☐ **арест** _(ar-yest)_ . . . . arrest _____
☐ **армия** _(ar-mee-yah)_ . . . . army **а** _____
☐ **аспирин** _(ah-spee-reen)_ . . . . aspirin _____
☐ **астронавт** _(ah-strah-nahvt)_ . . . . astronaut _____

13

(chyor-nee)
чёрный = black _____ **Это чёрный стол.**
(et-tah) (chyor-nee) (stohl)
that black table

(zhyol-tee)
жёлтый = yellow _____ **Это жёлтый банан.**
(et-tah) (zhyol-tee) (bah-nahn)
yellow banana

(see-nee)
синий = blue синий _____ **Это синий автомобиль.**
(see-nee) (ahv-tah-mah-beel)
blue car

(syeh-ree)
серый = gray _____ **Это серый слон.**
(syeh-ree) (slohn)
gray elephant

(byel-lee)
белый = white _____ **Это белый телефон.**
(byel-lee) (teh-leh-fohn)
white telephone

(krahs-nee)
красный = red _____ **Это красный автобус.**
(krahs-nee) (ahv-toh-boos)
red bus

(zyel-yoh-nee)
зелёный = green _____ **Это зелёный салат.**
(zyel-yoh-nee) (sah-laht)
green salad

(kah-reech-nyeh-vwee)
коричневый = brown _____ **Это коричневый стул.**
(kah-reech-nyeh-vwee) (stool)
brown chair

(roh-zah-vwee)
розовый = pink _____ **Это розовый цветок.**
(roh-zah-vwee) (tsvet-ohk)
pink flower

(oh-rahn-zheh-vwee)
оранжевый = orange _____ **Это оранжевый мяч.**
(oh-rahn-zheh-vwee) (mee-yahch)
orange ball

Now peel off the next **десять** labels **и** proceed to label these **цвета в** your **доме.**
(dyes-yet) ten *(ee)* *(tsvet-ah)* colors *(vuh)* in *(doh-myeh)* house

Now let's practice using these **слова.**
(slah-vah)

(gdyeh) (byel-lee) (teh-leh-fohn)
Где белый телефон? **Там белый _____ телефон.**
where is white telephone *(tahm)* there is *(teh-leh-fohn)* telephone

(gdyeh) (syeh-ree) (ahv-tah-mah-beel)
Где серый автомобиль? **Там_____ автомобиль.**
gray car *(tahm)* there is *(ahv-tah-mah-beel)* car

(gdyeh) (kah-reech-nyeh-vwee)(stool)
Где коричневый стул? **Вот _____ стул.**
brown chair *(voht)* here is *(stool)* chair

Где чёрный мяч? **Вот_____мяч.**
(chyor-nee) (mee-yahch) black ball *(voht)* here is *(mee-yahch)* ball

Где оранжевый кот? **Вот _____ кот.**
(oh-rahn-zheh-vwee)(koht) orange cat *(voht)* *(koht)* cat

(krahs-nee) (ahv-toh-boos)
Где красный автобус? **Там_____ автобус.**
red bus *(tahm)* *(ahv-toh-boos)* bus

(gdyeh) (zyel-yoh-nee) (beel-yet)   *(voht)*   *(beel-yet)*
Где зелёный билет?   **Вот** _____ **билет.**
  green   ticket

(roh-zah-vwee) (dohm)   *(tahm)*   *(dohm)*
Где розовый дом?   **Там** _____ **дом.**
  pink   house

(zhyol-tee) (bah-nahn)   *(voht)*   *(bah-nahn)*
Где жёлтый банан?   **Вот** _____ **банан.**
  yellow

(pah-roos-skee)
Note: **По-русски,** "I have" and "we have" are written as follows.

(oo) (men-yah) (yest)
у меня есть = I have _____

(oo)(nahs) (yest)
у нас есть = we have _____

(yah)(hah-choo)(koo-peet)   *(mwee) (hah-teem) (koo-peet)*   *(oo) (men-yah) (yest)*
Let's review „**я хочу купить**" and „**мы хотим купить**," and learn „**у меня есть**"
         I   would like   to buy   we   would like   to buy   I   have

(oo) (nahs)(yest)
and „**у нас есть.**" Repeat each sentence out loud over and over.
 we   have

(yah) (hah-choo)(koo-peet) (pee-vah)
Я хочу купить пиво.
I   would like   to buy   a beer

(oo) (men-yah) (yest) (pee-vah)
У меня есть пиво.
I   have   a beer

(mwee) (hah-teem) (koo-peet) (dvah)(stah-kah-nah)(vee-nah)
Мы хотим купить два стакана вина.
we   would like   two   glasses of   wine

(oo) (nahs) (yest) (dvah) (stah-kah-nah)(vee-nah)
У нас есть два стакана вина.
we   have   glasses of

(yah) (hah-choo)   *(sah-laht)*
Я хочу купить салат.
               a salad

(dohm)
У нас есть дом.
            a house

(mwee)   *(mar-ahk)*
Мы хотим купить семь марок.
                 stamps

(men-yah) (yest)   *(dohm) (vuh)(ah-myeh-ree-kyeh)*
У меня есть дом в Америке.
I   have   a house   in   America

(oo) (men-yah) (yest)   *(oo) (nahs) (yest)*   *(yah)(hah-choo) (koo-peet)*
Now fill in the following blanks with „**у меня есть**," „**у нас есть**," „**я хочу купить**"

(mwee) (hah-teem) (koo-peet)
or „**мы хотим купить.**"

У нас есть
              (we have)

(dyes-yet) (mah-rahk)
десять марок.
         stamps

_____
     (we would like to buy)

(dvah) (beel-yet-tah)
два билета.
      tickets

_____
         (I have)

(sah-laht)
салат.
salad

_____
     (I would like to buy)

(syem) (aht-krit-tahk)
семь открыток.
postcards

☐ **бал** *(bahl)*.	ball (dance)	
☐ **балалайка** *(bah-lah-lie-kah)*	balalaika	
☐ **балерина** *(bah-leh-ree-nah)*	ballerina	**б**
☐ **балет** *(bahl-yet)*.	ballet	
☐ **балкон** *(bahl-kohn)*.	balcony	

(teep-yair)
Теперь a quick review of *(tsvet-ohv)* **цветов.** Draw lines between the *(roos-skee-mee)* **русскими** *(slah-vah-mee)* **словами** *(ee)* **и** the
now   colors   Russian   words

correct *(tsvet-ah-mee)* **цветами.** On your mark, get set, *GO!*
        colors

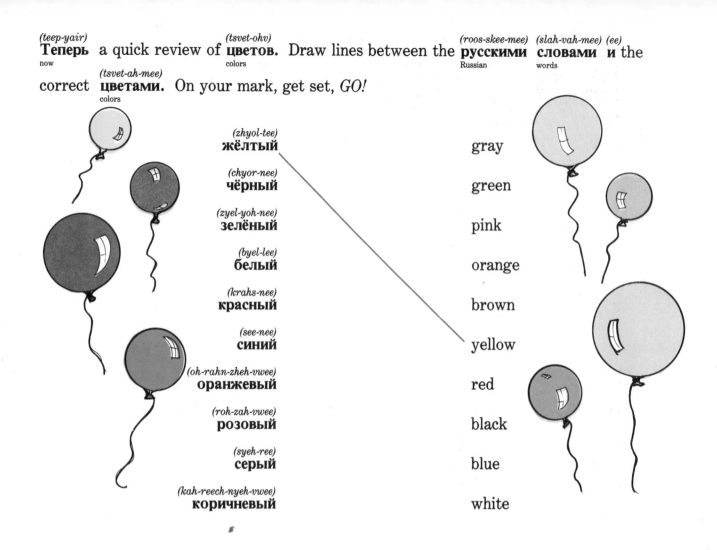

(zhyol-tee)
жёлтый   gray

(chyor-nee)
чёрный   green

(zyel-yoh-nee)
зелёный   pink

(byel-lee)
белый   orange

(krahs-nee)
красный   brown

(see-nee)
синий   yellow

(oh-rahn-zheh-vwee)
оранжевый   red

(roh-zah-vwee)
розовый   black

(syeh-ree)
серый   blue

(kah-reech-nyeh-vwee)
коричневый   white

(pah-roos-skee)
По-русски, the letter **е** is often pronounced *"yeh"* (as in the English word "yes.") When a
in   Russian

letter such as **н, д** or **п** precedes the *"yeh"* sound, they combine to make one sound.

For example, the *(roos-skoh-yeh)(sloh-vah)* **русское слово** for "no" is **„нет"** pronounced like the *(ahn-glee-skoh-yeh)* **английское** *(sloh-vah)* **слово**
                                Russian   word   English   word

"net" with a "y": *"nyet."* As you practice each of the following words, combine the sound

of *"yeh"* with the letter that precedes it, making one, smooth sound.

(gdyeh)
где
where

(zdyes)
здесь
here

(dyet-ee)
дети
children

(syem)
семь
seven

(dyev-yet)
девять
nine

(dyes-yet)
десять
ten

(kah-bee-nyet)
кабинет
study

(byel-lee)
белый
white

(syeh-ree)
серый
blue

☐ **банан** *(bah-nahn)* . . . . banana
☐ **бандит** *(bahn-deet)* . . . . bandit, robber
☐ **бар** *(bar)* . . . . bar (restaurant)
☐ **баржа** *(bar-zhah)* . . . . barge
☐ **барьер** *(bar-yair)* . . . . barrier

б

16

(dyen-gee)
Деньги
money

Before starting this Step, go back and review Step 4.   Make sure you can count to

(dvahd-tset)
двадцать without looking *(vuh)(kuh-nee-goo)* **в книгу.**   Let's learn the larger *(chee-slah)* **числа** now, so if something
twenty   at   the book   numbers

costs more than 20 *(roo-blay)* **рублей,** you will know exactly *(skohl-kah)* **сколько** it costs.   After practicing aloud
                         rubles

(roos-skee-yeh)
русские numbers 10 through 1000 below, write these *(chee-slah)* **числа** in the blanks provided.
Russian   numbers

Again, notice the similarities (underlined) between *(chee-slah-mee)* **числами** such as *(tree)* **три** (3), *(tree-nod-tset)* **тринадцать** (13)
                                                         numbers

and *(treed-tset)* **тридцать** (30).

10	*(dyes-yet)* **десять**	(пять + пять = десять)		10	ДЕСЯТЬ
20	*(dvahd-tset)* **двадцать**		(**два** = 2)	20	
30	*(treed-tset)* **тридцать**		(**три** = 3)	30	
40	*(so-rahk)* **сорок**	*(cheh-tir-ee)* (**четыре** = 4)		40	
50	*(peed-dyes-yaht)* **пятьдесят**	*(pyaht)* (**пять** = 5)		50	
60	*(shest-dyes-yaht)* **шестьдесят**	(**шесть** = 6)		60	
70	*(syem-dyes-yet)* **семьдесят**	(**семь** = 7)		70	
80	*(voh-syem-dyes-yet)* **восемьдесят**	(**восемь** = 8)		80	
90	*(dyev-yah-noh-stah)* **девяносто**	*(dyev-yet)* (**девять** = 9)		90	
100	*(stoh)* **сто**			100	
500	*(pyet-soht)* **пятьсот**			500	
1000	*(tee-seh-chah)* **тысяча**			1000	

Now take a logical guess. *(kahk)* **Как** would you write *(ee)* **и** say the following? *(aht-vyet-ee)* **Ответы** are at
                               how   and   the answers

the bottom of *(strah-neet-sih)* **страницы.**
                 the page

140 _____   52 _____

610 _____   1100 _____

The unit of currency **в** *(vuh)* in **Советском** *(sah-vyet-skahm)* the Soviet **Союзе** *(sah-yoo-zeh)* Union is the **рубль,** abbreviated **руб.** or **р.** Bills are called **рубли** *(roo-blee)* **и** *(ee)* and coins are called **копейки,** *(kah-pay-kee)* abbreviated **коп.** Just as **американский** *(ah-myeh-ree-kahn-skee)* an American **или** *(ee-lee)* **канадский** *(kah-nahd-skee)* Canadian **доллар** *(dohl-lar)* dollar can be broken down into 100 pennies, а **рубль** *(roo-bil)* can be broken down into 100 **копеек.** *(kah-pyeh-eek)* Let's learn the various kinds of **рублей** *(roo-blay)* **и** *(ee)* **копеек.** *(kah-pyeh-eek)* Always be sure to practice each **слово** *(slah-vah)* out loud. You will not be able to exchange money before your arrival **в** *(vuh)* in **Советском Союзе,** *(sah-vyet-skahm) (sah-yoo-zeh)* so take a few minutes now to familiarize yourself with Russian currency.

Рубли *(roo-blee)*
rubles

один рубль *(ah-deen) (roo-bil)*
one

три рубля *(tree) (roob-lyah)*
three

пять рублей *(pyaht) (roo-blay)*
five

десять рублей *(dyes-yet) (roo-blay)*
ten

Монеты *(mohn-yet-ee)*
coins

Серебро *(seh-reh-broh)*
silver coins

десять копеек *(dyes-yet) (kah-pyeh-eek)*
ten

пятнадцать копеек *(pyaht-nod-tset) (kah-pyeh-eek)*
fifteen

двадцать копеек *(dvahd-tset) (kah-pyeh-eek)*
twenty

пятьдесят копеек *(peed-dyes-yaht)*
fifty

Медь *(mee-yed)*
copper coins

одна копейка *(ahd-nah)(kah-pay-kah)*
one

две копейки *(dveh) (kah-pay-kee)*
two

три копейки *(tree) (kah-pay-kee)*
three

пять копеек *(pyaht) (kah-pyeh-eek)*
five

☐ **бас** *(bahs)*........................	bass (voice)
☐ **баскетбол** *(bah-sket-bohl)*..................	basketball
☐ **батальон** *(bah-tahl-yohn)*.................	battalion
☐ **батарея** *(bah-tar-yeh-yah)*...............	battery
☐ **Бельгия** *(byel-gee-yah)*..............	Belgium

б

Review **числа десять** *(chee-slah) (dyes-yet)* through **тысяча** *(tee-seh-chah)* again. **Теперь, как** *(teep-yair) (kahk)* do you say "twenty-two"
the numbers ten · one thousand · now · how

или *(ee-lee)* "fifty-three" **по-русски?** *(pah-roos-skee)* You basically put the numbers together in a logical sequence.
or

For example, 78 (70 + 8) = **семьдесят** *(syem-dyes-yet)* **восемь.** *(voh-syem)* See if you can say **и** *(ee)* write out **числа** *(chee-slah)*
seventy · eight · and · the numbers

on this **странице.** *(strah-neet-seh)* **Ответы** *(aht-vyet-ee)* are at the bottom of **страницы.** *(strah-neet-sih)*
page · answers

a. 25 = _____ (20 + 5)		e. 36 = *Тридцать шесть* (30 + 6)
b. 47 = _____ (40 + 7)		f. 93 = _____ (90 + 3)
c. 84 = _____ (80 + 4)		g. 68 = _____ (60 + 8)
d. 51 = _____ (50 + 1)		h. 72 = _____ (70 + 2)

To ask how much something costs **по-русски,** *(pah-roos-skee)* one asks „**Сколько это стоит**" *(skohl-kah) (et-tah) (stoy-eet)* **Теперь** *(teep-yair)*
now

answer the following questions based on **числа** *(chee-slah)* in parentheses.
the numbers

1. **Сколько это стоит?** *(skohl-kah) (et-tah) (stoy-eet)*
   how much · this · costs
   Это стоит *(et-tah)(stoy-eet)* _____ **рублей.** *(roo-blay)*
   this · costs · (10) · rubles

2. **Сколько это стоит?**
   Это стоит *Пять* _____ **рублей.** *(roo-blay)*
   (5)

3. **Сколько стоит книга?** *(stoy-eet) (kuh-nee-gah)*
   costs · the book
   Книга стоит *(kuh-nee-gah)* _____ **рублей.** *(roo-blay)*
   (17)

4. **Сколько стоит карта?** *(kar-tah)*
   the map
   Карта стоит _____ **рублей.**
   (6)

5. **Сколько стоит картина?** *(kar-tee-nah)*
   the picture
   Картина стоит _____ **рублей.**
   (110)

6. **Сколько стоит банан?** *(bah-nahn)*
   the banana
   Банан стоит _____ **копеек.** *(kah-pyeh-eek)*
   (20) · kopecks

7. **Сколько стоит открытка?** *(aht-krit-kah)*
   the postcard
   Открытка стоит _____ **копеек.** *(kah-pyeh-eek)*
   (12)

19

Step 7

(see-vohd-nyah) *(zahv-trah)* *(ee)* *(vchee-rah)*
Сегодня, Завтра и Вчера
today   tomorrow   and   yesterday

(kah-leen-dar)
Календарь
calendar

(syem) *(dnay)* *(nee-dyel-yeh)*
Семь дней в неделе.
seven days in week

(pah-nee-dyel-neek) понедельник Monday	*(vtor-neek)* вторник Tuesday	*(sree-dah)* среда Wednesday	*(chet-vyairg)* четверг Thursday	*(pyaht-neet-sah)* пятница Friday	*(soo-boh-tah)* суббота Saturday	*(voh-skree-syen-yah)* воскресенье Sunday
1	2	3	4	5	6	7

(oh-cheen) *(vazh-nah)*
Очень важно to know the days of the week **и** the various parts of the day. Let's learn
it is very important   *(ee)*

them. Be sure to say them aloud before filling in the blanks below. **Русские** begin
(roos-skee-yeh)
Russians

counting their week on Monday with „**понедельник.**"
(pah-nee-dyel-neek)

(pah-nee-dyel-neek)
понедельник _____

(vtor-neek)
вторник _____

(sree-dah)
среда _среда, среда_

(chet-vyairg)
четверг _____

(pyaht-neet-sah)
пятница _____

(soo-boh-tah)
суббота _____

(voh-skree-syen-yah)
воскресенье _____

Monday / Tuesday / Wednesday / Thursday / Friday / Saturday / Sunday

---

(see-vohd-nyah) *(sree-dah)* *(zahv-trah)* *(boo-dyet)* *(chet-vyairg)* *(vchee-rah)* *(bil)* *(vtor-neek)*
If **сегодня среда,** then **завтра будет четверг** and **вчера был вторник.**
today   Wednesday   tomorrow will be Thursday   yesterday was Tuesday

(teep-yair)
Теперь you supply the correct answers. If **сегодня понедельник,** then **завтра будет**
now   *(see-vohd-nyah)* *(pah-nee-dyel-neek)* *(zahv-trah)* *(boo-dyet)*
                                                  today   Monday   tomorrow

_____ and **вчера был** _____. Or, if **сегодня**
                      (vchee-rah) *(bil)*   *(see-vohd-nyah)*
                      yesterday was   today

(pah-nee-dyel-neek)
понедельник, then _завтра_ **будет вторник** and _____
Monday   *(boo-dyet)* *(vtor-neek)*
                              will be Tuesday

(bil) *(voh-skree-syen-yah)* *(chtoh)* *(see-vohd-nyah)*
был воскресенье. Что сегодня? Сегодня _____.
                    what is today

(teep-yair) *(syem)* *(kah-leen-dar)*
Теперь, peel off the next **семь** labels **и** put them on **календарь** you use every day.
now   calendar

From now on, Monday is **понедельник.** Notice that Friday—**пятница**—is the fifth day of
                        (pah-nee-dyel-neek)   *(pyaht-neet-sah)*

the week **и** contains the **слово** for five—**пять.**
                                              (pyaht)

☐ **Библия** *(bee-blee-yah)*	Bible	
☐ **бинокль** *(bee-noh-kil)*	binoculars	
☐ **бланк** *(blahnk)*	blank (form)	**б**
☐ **бокс** *(bohks)*	boxing	
☐ **Болгария** *(bahl-gar-ee-yah)*	Bulgaria	

There are **четыре** *(cheh-tir-ee)* parts to each **день.** *(dyen)*
four   day

morning = **утро** *(oo-trah)*	УТРО, УТРО, УТРО
afternoon/daytime = **день** *(dyen)*	
evening = **вечер** *(vyeh-cher)*	
night = **ночь** *(nohch)*	

Notice that „в" means "on." For example, „в воскресенье *(voh-skree-syen-yah)* утром *(oo-trahm)*" means on Sunday morning." **Теперь,** *(teep-yair)* fill in the following blanks **и** then check your answers at the bottom of
now
страницы. *(strah-neet-sih)* Don't be surprised that the words change slightly.
page

a.	on Sunday morning	= В ВОСКРЕСЕНЬЕ УТРОМ
b.	on Friday morning	= В
c.	on Friday evening	= В
d.	on Saturday evening	=
e.	on Saturday morning	=
f.	on Wednesday morning	=
g.	on Wednesday afternoon	=
h.	on Thursday afternoon	=
i.	on Thursday evening	=
j.	yesterday evening	= ВЧЕРА ВЕЧЕРОМ
k.	yesterday afternoon	=
l.	yesterday morning	=
m.	tomorrow morning	=
n.	tomorrow afternoon	=

ОТВЕТЫ

a.	в воскресенье утром	f.	в среду утром	k.	вчера днём
b.	в пятницу утром	g.	в среду днём	l.	вчера утром
c.	в пятницу вечером	h.	в четверг днём	m.	завтра утром
d.	в субботу вечером	i.	в четверг вечером	n.	завтра днём
e.	в субботу утром	j.	вчера вечером		

So, with merely eleven **слова**, you can specify any **день** of **недели** и any time of **дня**.
(slah-vah) words — *(dyen)* day — *(nee-dyel-ee)* week — *(den-yah)* day

Сегодня, завтра и вчера will be **очень важные слова** for you in making reservations и
(see-vohd-nyah) today — *(zahv-trah)* tomorrow — *(vchee-rah)* yesterday — *(oh-cheen)* very — *(vazh-nih-yeh)* important

appointments, in getting **билеты** for **театр** и for many other things you will want to do.
(beel-yet-tee) tickets — *(tee-ah-ter)* theater

Knowing the parts of **дня** will help you to learn и understand the various **русские**
(den-yah) day — and — *(roos-skee-yeh)* Russian

greetings below. Practice these every day until your trip.

good morning	=	**доброе утро** *(doh-brah-yeh)(oo-trah)*
good day good afternoon	=	**добрый день** *(doh-brih) (dyen)*
good evening	=	**добрый вечер** *(doh-brih) (vyeh-cher)*
good night	=	**спокойной ночи** *(spah-koy-nih) (noh-chee)*
How are you?	=	**Как дела?** *(kahk) (dee-lah)*

добрый вечер

Notice that "good afternoon" and "good day" are the same **по-русски**: „**доброе утро**"?
(doh-brah-yeh)(oo-trah)

Take the next **четыре** labels и stick them on the appropriate things in your **доме**.
(cheh-tir-ee) four — *(doh-mee)* house

How about the bathroom mirror for „**доброе утро**"? **Или** the front door for
(doh-brah-yeh)(oo-trah) — *(ee-lee)* or

„**добрый день**"? **Или** your alarm clock for „**спокойной ночи**"? **Или** your kitchen cabinet
(doh-brih) (dyen) — *(ee-lee)* or — *(spah-koy-nih) (noh-chee)*

for „**Как дела**"? You are about one-fourth of your way through **эту книгу** и it is a good
(kahk) (dee-lah) — *(et-too) (kuh-nee-goo)* this book

time to quickly review **слова** you have learned before doing the crossword puzzle on the

next **странице. Удачи! Или,** as we say **по-английски**, "good luck to you!"
(strah-neet-seh) page — *(oo-dah-chee)* — *(pah-ahn-glee-skee)* in English

CROSSWORD PUZZLE

ACROSS

1. bank
3. hotel/inn
6. to buy
8. page
10. no
12. kitchen
13. wall
14. green
15. two
16. Soviet Union
21. orange
23. where
25. kopecks
27. costs
28. why
30. postcard
32. lamp
34. dollar
36. coffee
37. fourteen
39. morning
40. picture
43. table
44. this

DOWN

2. when
4. telephone
5. taxi
6. brown
7. toilet
9. banana
11. American
12. who
17. blue
18. curtain
19. fifteen
20. door
22. automobile
24. how much
26. how
29. one
31. mail
33. five
35. or
36. red
38. color
41. zero
42. window

Step 8

(vuh) *(nah)* *(pohd)*
В, На, Под...
in   on   under

(roos-skee-yeh)
Русские prepositions (words like "in," "on," "through" and "next to") are easy to learn **и** *(ee)*
Russian

they allow you to be precise **с** a minimum of effort. Instead of having to point **шесть** *(shest)*
(suh) with   six

times at a piece of yummy pastry you would like, you can explain precisely which one

you want by saying it is behind, in front of, next to **или** under the piece of pastry that
(ee-lee)

the salesperson is starting to pick up. Let's learn some of these **маленькие слова** by
(mah-leen-kee-ee)
little   words

studying **примеры** below.
(pree-myeh-rih)
examples

(eez)
из = out of/from   *(ryah-dahm) (suh)*   **под** = under
(vuh)   **рядом   с** = next to   *(pohd)*
в = into/in   **над** = over
                                                                            (nahd)

(moozh-chee-nah)(vih-shlah) (eez) (gah-stee-neet-sih)
Мужчина вышла из гостиницы.
man   comes   out of

(zhen-shchee-nah) (ee-dyoht) (vuh) (gah-stee-neet-soo)
Женщина   идёт   в   гостиницу.
woman   goes   into hotel

(vrahch) (vuh) (gah-stee-neet-syeh)
Врач в   гостинице.
doctor (is) in hotel

(kar-tee-nah) (nahd) (stah-lohm)
Картина над   столом.
picture   (is) over table

(kar-tee-nah) (ryah-dahm) (suh)(chah-sah-mee)
Картина рядом   с   часами.
picture   (is) next to   clock

(sah-bah-kah)(pohd) (stah-lohm)
Собака под   столом.
dog   (is) under

(chah-see)   (stah-lohm)
Часы над столом.
clock   (is) over

(ryah-dahm) (suh)(kar-tee-noy)
Часы рядом   с   картиной.
           (is) next to   picture

Fill in the blanks below **с** *(suh)* / with the correct prepositions according to **картинкам** *(kar-teen-kahm)* / pictures on the previous **странице.** *(strah-neet-seh)* / page

Мужчина *(moozh-chee-nah)* / man **вышла** *(vih-shlah)* / comes _____ (out of) **гостиницы.** *(gah-stee-neet-sih)*

Собака *(sah-bah-kah)* / dog ___ ПОД ___ (under) **столом.** *(stah-lohm)* / table

Часы *(chah-see)* / clock _____ (over) **столом.** / table

Врач *(vrahch)* / doctor _____ (in) **гостинице.** *(gah-stee-neet-syeh)*

Часы _____ (next to) **картиной.** *(kar-tee-noy)* / picture

Картина / picture _____ (over) **столом.**

Стол / table _____ (under) **картиной.**

Картина / picture _____ (next to) **часами.** *(chah-sah-mee)* / clock

Женщина *(zhen-shchee-nah)* / woman **идёт** *(ee-dyoht)* / goes _____ (into) **гостиницу.** *(gah-stee-neet-soo)*

Стол _____ (under) **часами.**

Теперь, *(teep-yair)* / now answer **вопросы** *(vah-proh-see)* / questions based on **картинках** *(kar-teen-kahk)* / pictures on the previous **странице.** *(strah-neet-seh)* / page

Где *(gdyeh)* **врач?** *(vrahch)* / doctor _____

Где собака? *(sah-bah-kah)* / dog *Собака под столом.*

Где стол? / table _____

Где картина? *(kar-tee-nah)* / picture _____

Что *(chtoh)* / what **делает** *(dyeh-lah-yet)* / does **эта женщина?** *(zhen-shchee-nah)* / woman _____

Что делает *(dyeh-lah-yet)* / does **этот** *(et-tut)* / this **мужчина?** *(moozh-chee-nah)* / man _____

Часы *(chah-see)* / (is) clock **зелёные?** *(zyel-yoh-nih-yeh)* / green _____

Собака / (is) dog **серая?** *(syeh-rah-yah)* / gray _____

☐ **бульвар** *(bool-var)* .... boulevard _____
☐ **бюрократ** *(byoo-rah-kraht)* .... bureaucrat _____
☐ **ваза** *(vah-zah)* .... vase _____
☐ **вальс** *(vahls)* .... waltz _____
☐ **Ватикан** *(vah-tee-kahn)* .... Vatican _____

В

(teep-yair)
Теперь for some more practice with **русскими** prepositions!
now   *(roos-skee-mee)* Russian

(nah)
на = on

(myezh-doo)
между = between

(pyeh-red)
перед = in front of

(zah)
за = behind

(stah-kahn) (voh-dih) (nah) (stohl-yeh)
Стакан воды на столе.
glass   of water   (is) on   table

(kar-tee-nah)   *(styen-yeh)*
Картина на стене.
picture   (is) on   wall

(lahm-pah) (zah) (stah-lohm)
Лампа за столом.
lamp   (is) behind   table

(stohl) (pyeh-red) (kroh-vaht-yoo)
Стол перед кроватью.
table   (is) in front of   bed

(lahm-pah) (myezh-doo)   *(kroh-vaht-yoo)*
Лампа между столом и кроватью.
lamp   (is) between   table   and   bed

(stah-kahn) (voh-dih)
Стакан воды ___на_____ **столе.**
                          table

Картина_____**стене.**
                          wall

Лампа_____**столом.**
                          table

(kroh-vaht-yoo)
Стол _____**кроватью.**
                          bed

Лампа _____ **столом и кроватью.**

Answer the following **вопросы**, based on **картинках**, by filling in the blanks **с** the correct
          (vah-proh-see)   *(kar-teen-kahk)*   *(suh)*
          questions   pictures

prepositions. Choose the prepositions from those you have just learned.

(gdyeh) (kuh-nee-gah)
Где книга?
book

Книга _____ **столе.**
                   (on)   *(stohl-yeh)*

(ahv-toh-boos)
Где автобус?
bus

Автобус _____ **гостиницей.**
                 (in front of)   *(gah-stee-neet-say)* hotel

☐ **веранда** *(vee-rahn-dah)* . . . . veranda
☐ **витамин** *(vee-tah-meen)* . . . . vitamin
☐ **водка** *(vohd-kah)* . . . . vodka   **В**
☐ **волейбол** *(voh-lay-bohl)* . . . . volleyball
☐ **Волга** *(vohl-gah)* . . . . Volga River

(teh-leh-fohn) Где **телефон?** Где **ковёр?** Где **картина?**
telephone   *(kahv-yor)* carpet   picture

(syeh-ree)   *(styen-yeh)*
Серый телефон _____ **стене.**
gray   (on)   wall

                                            (kar-tee-noy)
Серый телефон РЯДОМ С **картиной.**
                                 (next to)   picture

                                            (stah-lohm)
Серый телефон _____ **столом.**
                                   (over)   table

(zyel-yoh-nee) (kahv-yor)
Зелёный ковёр _____ **столом.**
green   carpet   (under)

Картина _____ **стене.**
picture   (on)

(teep-yair)   *(gah-stee-neet-seh)*   *(suh)*
Теперь, fill in each blank on **гостинице** below **с** the best possible preposition.
now   hotel

          (aht-vyet-ee)   *(strah-neet-sih)*
The correct **ответы** are at the bottom of **страницы.** Have fun!
             answers   page

1. _____

3. _____

6. НА _____

5. _____

2. _____

4. _____

10. _____

8. _____

9. _____

7. _____

Step 9

(vuh) *(yahn-var-yeh)* *(fyev-rahl-yeh)* *(mart-yeh)*
В Январе, Феврале, Марте
in January February March

(treed-tset) *(dnay)* *(syen-tyah-bree-yeh)* *(ahp-ryel-yeh)*
Тридцать дней в сентябре, апреле,
thirty days September April

(ee-yoon-yeh) *(nah-yah-bree-yeh)*
июне, и ноябре.
June November

Sound familiar? You have learned **дни** *(dnee)* **недели,** *(nee-dyel-ee)* so now it is time to learn **месяцы** *(myes-yet-see)* **года** *(go-dah)*
days of week months of year

и all the different kinds of **погоды.** *(pah-go-dih)* **Например,** *(nah-pree-myair)* you ask about the **погоде** *(pah-go-dyeh)* **по-русски** *(pah-roos-skee)* just
weather for example weather in Russian

as you would **по-английски:** *(pah-ahn-glee-skee)* „**Какая** *(kah-kah-yah)* **сегодня** *(see-vohd-nyah)* **погода?"** *(pah-go-dah)* Practice all the possible
how is today weather

answers to this **вопрос** *(vah-prohs)* **и тогда** *(tahg-dah)* write the answers in the blanks below.
question then

(kah-kah-yah) *(see-vohd-nyah)* *(pah-go-dah)*
Какая сегодня погода?

(see-vohd-nyah) *(ee-dyoht)* *(dohzhd)*
Сегодня идёт дождь. _____
today it is raining

(ee-dyoht) *(snyeg)*
Сегодня идёт снег. _____
it is snowing

(zhar-kah)
Сегодня жарко. _____
hot

(hoh-lahd-nah)
Сегодня холодно. *Сегодня жарко.* _____
cold

(hah-roh-shah-yah)(pah-go-dah)
Сегодня хорошая погода. _____
good weather

(plah-hah-yah)(pah-go-dah)
Сегодня плохая погода. _____
bad weather

(too-mahn)
Сегодня туман. _____
foggy

(vyet-rin-oh)
Сегодня ветрено. _____
windy

(tyep-loh)
Сегодня тепло. _____
warm

(teep-yair) **Теперь,** practice **слова** on the next **странице** *(strah-neet-seh)* **и тогда** *(tahg-dah)* fill in the blanks **с** *(suh)* the names
now then

(myes-yet-sev) **месяцев и** the appropriate weather reports.
of months

☐ **газ** *(gahz)* .... natural gas
☐ **газета** *(gah-zyet-ah)* .... gazette, newspaper
☐ —**газетчик** *(gah-zyet-cheek)* .... newspaper man
☐ **галерея** *(gahl-yair-eh-yah)* .... gallery **Г**
28 ☐ **генерал** *(gee-nee-rahl)* .... general

_____
_____
_____
_____
_____

(vuh) *(yahn-var-yeh)*		*(vuh)* *(ee-dyoht)* *(snyeg)*	
В **январе** _____		**В январе идёт снег.** _____	
in January		in January it is snowing	

(vuh) *(yahn-var-yeh)*
В **январе** _____
in   January

(fyev-rahl-yeh)
В **феврале** _____
February

(mart-yeh)
В **марте** _____
March

(ahp-ryel-yeh)
В **апреле** _____
April

(mah-yeh)
В **мае** В мае _____
May

(ee-yoon-yeh)
В **июне** _____
June

(vuh) *(ee-yool-yeh)*
В **июле** _____
July

(ahv-goost-yeh)
В **августе** _____
August

(syen-tyah-bree-yeh)
В **сентябре** _____
September

(ahk-tyah-bree-yeh)
В **октябре** _____
October

(nah-yah-bree-yeh)
В **ноябре** _____
November

(dee-kah-bree-yeh)
В **декабре** _____
December

(vuh) *(ee-dyoht)* *(snyeg)*
В январе идёт снег. _____
in January   it is   snowing

(fyev-rahl-yeh)
В феврале идёт снег. _____
February   it is   snowing

(dohzhd)
В марте идёт дождь. _____
it is   raining

(dohzhd)
В апреле идёт дождь. _____

(vyet-rin-oh)
В мае ветрено. _____
windy

(vyet-rin-oh)
В июне ветрено. _____
June

(zhar-kah)
В июле жарко. В июле жарко.
hot

В августе жарко. _____
hot

(hah-roh-shah-yah) *(pah-go-dah)*
В сентябре хорошая погода. _____
September   good   weather

(too-mahn)
В октябре туман. _____
foggy

(hoh-lahd-nah)
В ноябре холодно. _____
cold

(plah-hah-yah)
В декабре плохая погода. _____
bad

(teep-yair) *(vah-proh-see)* *(kar-teen-kahk)*
Теперь, answer the following **вопросы** based on **картинках** to the right.
questions   pictures

(kah-kah-yah) *(pah-go-dah)* *(vuh)* *(fyev-rahl-yeh)*
Какая погода в феврале? _____
how is   February

(ahp-ryel-yeh)
Какая погода в апреле? В апреле идёт дождь.
April

(mah-yeh)
Какая погода в мае? _____
May

(ahv-goost-yeh)
Какая погода в августе? _____

(see-vohd-nyah) *(hah-roh-shah-yah)* *(plah-hah-yah)*
Какая погода сегодня? Хорошая или плохая? _____
bad

☐ **Греция** *(gret-see-yah)* .... Greece		_____
—where they speak **по-гречески** *(pah-greh-chee-skee)*		
☐ **география** *(gee-ah-grah-fee-yah)* .... geography	**Г**	_____
☐ **геология** *(gee-oh-loh-gee-yah)* .... geology		_____
☐ —**геолог** *(gee-oh-lohg)* .... geologist		_____

Теперь for the seasons of **года...**
year

(zee-moy) **зимой** in winter	*(lyet-ahm)* **летом** in summer	*(oh-seen-yoo)* **осенью** in autumn	*(vees-noy)* **весной** in spring

Зимой холодно

(zee-moy) (hoh-lahd-nah) **Зимой холодно.**	*(lyet-ahm) (zhar-kah)* **Летом жарко.**	*(oh-seen-yoo) (vyet-rin-oh)* **Осенью ветрено.** windy	*(vees-noy) (ee-dyoht)* **Весной идёт дождь.**

At this point, it is **хорошая** idea to familiarize yourself **с**
(hah-roh-shah-yah)
good
русскими температурами.
(suh) (roos-skee-mee) (teem-pee-rah-too-rah-mee)
temperatures

Read the typical weather forecasts below **и** carefully study the thermometer because

температуры в Советском Союзе are calculated on the basis of Celsius (not
(teem-pee-rah-too-rih) (vuh) (sah-vyet-skahm) (sah-yoo-zeh)
temperatures

Fahrenheit).

(fah-ren-gate) **фаренгейт** Fahrenheit	*(tsel-see)* **цельси** Celsius	
212° F ——	100° C	*(teem-pee-rah-too-rah)(kee-pyeh-nee-yah)* **температура кипения** boiling point
98.6° F ——	37° C	*(nar-mahl-nah-yah)* **температура нормальная** normal
68° F ——	20° C	
32° F ——	0° C	*(zah-meer-zah-nee-yah)* **температура замерзания** freezing point
0° F ——	-17.8° C	
-10° F ——	-23.3° C	

Температура в Ленинграде:
(teem-pee-rah-too-rah) (lee-neen-grahd-yeh)
Leningrad

(hoh-lahd-nah) **холодно.**
cold

температура: пять градусов
(grah-doo-sohv)
temperature · five · degrees

Температура в Москве:
(mohsk-vyeh)
Moscow

(zhar-kah) **жарко**
hot

температура: двадцать градусов
(dvahd-tset)
twenty

Г

(seem-yah)	*(koohk-nyah)*	*(tsair-kahv)*	*(dyet-ee)*
Семья:	**Кухня,**	**Церковь,** и	**Дети**
family	kitchen	church	children

One of the charming aspects в *(vuh)(sah-vyet-skahm)* **Советском** *(sah-yoo-zeh)* **Союзе**

concerns names. A father's first name becomes the

middle name for both his sons и daughters.

Daughters add **-овна,** *(ohv-nah)* **-евна,** *(eev-nah)* or **-ична** *(eech-nah)* to the father's

first name и sons add **-ович** *(oh-veech)* **-евич** *(ee-veech)* or **-ич.** *(eech)* Both the

given first name и the father's name (patronymic) are constantly used **по-русски.** *(pah-roos-skee)* Mastering

these will help you master the language. Study **картинки** *(kar-teen-kee)* below и **тогда** *(tahg-dah)* practice these new

pictures   then

names on the next **странице.** *(strah-neet-seh)*

Семья

(ahn-nah)(pee-trohv-nah)
Анна Петровна

(nee-koh-lie) (bah-ree-so-veech)
Николай Борисович

(gleb) *(vlah-dee-mee-roh-veech)*
Глеб Владимирович

(mah-ree-yah)(nee-koh-lah-eev-nah)
Мария Николаевна

(ee-vahn) *(nee-koh-lah-eev-eech)*
Иван Николаевич

(nee-nah) *(ah-lek-say-yev-nah)*
Нина Алексейевна

(mee-hah-eel) *(gleb-oh-veech)*
Михаил Глебович

(tah-mah-rah) *(gleb-ohv-nah)*
Тамара Глебовна

(oh-leg) *(ee-vahn-oh-veech)*
Олег Иванович

(zee-nah-ee-dah) *(ee-vahn-nohv-nah)*
Зинаида Ивановна

☐ **грамм** *(grahm)*	gram		
☐ **гранит** *(grah-neet)*	granite	**Г**	
☐ **группа** *(groop-pah)*	group		
☐ **ГУМ** *(goom)*	department store in Moscow		
☐ **гусь** *(goose)*	goose		

(rohd-stveen-nee-kee)
родственники
relatives

(rah-dee-tee-lee)
родители
parents

(dyed)
дед _____
grandfather

(aht-yets)
отец _____
father

(bah-boosh-kah)
бабушка_____
grandmother

(maht)
мать _____
mother

(dyet-ee)
дети
children

(rohd-stveen-nee-kee)
родственники
relatives

(sin)
сын сын, сын, сын, сын
son

(dyah-dyah)
дядя _____
uncle

(dohch)
дочь _____
daughter

(tyoh-tyah)
тётя _____
aunt

(sin) *(dohch)* *(braht)* *(see-strah)*
Сын и дочь = брат и сестра!
                brother   sister

Let's learn how to identify *(seem-yah)* **семья** by name. Study the following examples carefully.
                                    family

(kahk) *(zah-voot)* *(aht-tsah)*
Как зовут отца?
how   is called   father

(aht-tsah) *(zah-voot)*
Отца зовут Иван Николаевич .
father   is called

(kahk) *(zah-voot)* *(maht)*
Как зовут мать?
how   is called   mother

(zah-voot)
Мать зовут Нина Алексейевна.
mother   is called

(kahk) *(zah-voot)* *(sin-ah)*
Как зовут сына?
how   is called   son

Сына зовут _____
              is called

(kahk) *(zah-voot)* *(dohch)*
Как зовут дочь?
how   is called   daughter

Дочь зовут _____
              is called

(zah-voot) *(dyed-ah)*
Как зовут деда?
how   is called   grandfather

Деда зовут _____
              is called

(bah-boosh-koo)
Как зовут бабушку?
grandmother

Бабушку зовут _____

(vahs) *(zah-voot)*
Как вас зовут?
how   are you called

(men-yah) *(zah-voot)*
Меня зовут _____
I am called   (your name)

☐ **дама** *(dah-mah)* . . . . dame, lady, woman
☐ **дата** *(dah-tah)* . . . . date
☐ **Дания** *(dah-nee-yah)* . . . . Denmark
☐ —where they speak **по-датски** *(pah-daht-skee)*
☐ **делегат** *(dyel-eh-gaht)* . . . . delegate

Д

_____
_____
_____
_____

32

(koohk-nyah)
Кухня
kitchen

Study all these *(kar-teen-kee)* **картинки** **и** then

practice saying *(ee)* **и** writing out **слова.**

(koohk-nyah)
Это кухня.
kitchen

(hah-lah-deel-neek)
ХОЛОДИЛЬНИК
refrigerator

_____

(plee-tah)
ПЛИТА
stove

_____

(vee-noh)
ВИНО
wine

_____

(pee-vah)
ПИВО
beer

_____

(mah-lah-koh)
МОЛОКО
milk

_____

(mah-slah)
масло
butter

масло
_____

(vah-proh-see)
Answer these вопросы aloud.
questions

(gdyeh) (pee-vah)
Где пиво? . . . . *(vuh)(hah-lah-deel-neek-yeh)* **Пиво в холодиильнике.**
beer   refrigerator

(mah-lah-koh)
Где молоко?
milk

(vee-noh)
Где вино?
wine

(bah-nahn)
Где банан?

(mah-slah)
Где масло?
butter

(sah-laht)
Где салат?
salad

(ah-bree-koh-see)
Где абрикосы?
apricots

☐ **демонстрация** *(dyeh-mahn-straht-see-yah)* . . . demonstration   _____
☐ **джаз** *(dzhahz)* . . . . jazz   _____
☐ **джин** *(dzheen)* . . . . gin   **Д**   _____
☐ **диагноз** *(dee-ahg-nohz)* . . . . diagnosis   _____
☐ **диаграмма** *(dee-ah-grahm-mah)* . . . . diagram, blueprint   _____

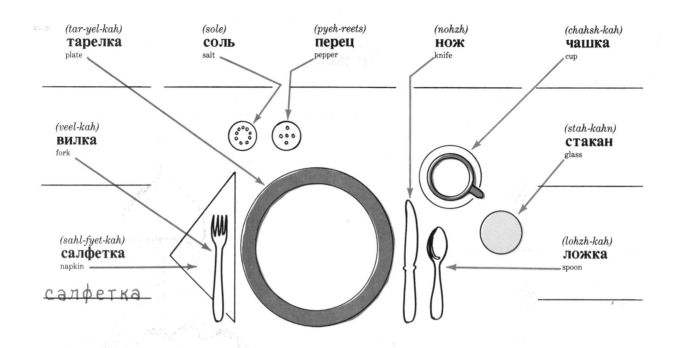

(tar-yel-kah)
тарелка
plate

(sole)
соль
salt

(pyeh-reets)
перец
pepper

(nohzh)
нож
knife

(chahsh-kah)
чашка
cup

(veel-kah)
вилка
fork

(stah-kahn)
стакан
glass

(sahl-fyet-kah)
салфетка
napkin

салфетка

(lohzh-kah)
ложка
spoon

И more…

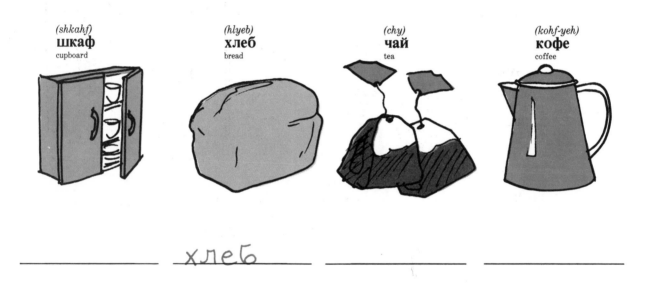

(shkahf)
шкаф
cupboard

(hlyeb)
хлеб
bread

(chy)
чай
tea

(kohf-yeh)
кофе
coffee

_____   хлеб   _____   _____

(gdyeh) (hlyeb) *(vuh)* *(hah-lah-deel-neek-yeh)* *(chy)* *(kohf-yeh)* *(kuh-nee-goo)*
Где хлеб? Хлеб в холодильнике. Где чай? Где кофе? Теперь open your **книгу**
bread   in   refrigerator   tea   coffee   book

(nah) (strah-neet-seh) (suh) *(div-yet-nod-tset)*
на странице с the labels **и** remove the next **девятнадцать** labels **и** proceed to label
to

(koohk-nyeh)
all these things in your **кухне.** Do not forget to use every opportunity to say these **слова**
kitchen

(oh-cheen) (vazh-nah)
out loud. **Это очень важно.**
very   important

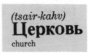

(tsair-kahv)
Церковь
church

(vuh) (sah-vyet-skahm) *(sah-yoo-zeh)* *(ree-lee-gee-ee)* *(ree-lee-gee-yah)*
В Советском Союзе, there is a wide variety of **религий**. A person's **религия** is
religions religion

usually one of the following.

(prah-vah-slahv-nah-yah) (prah-vah-slahv-nee)
1. **православная / православный** _____
Orthodox woman Orthodox man

(eev-ray-kah) (eev-ray)
2. **еврейка / еврей** _____
Jewish woman Jewish man

(kah-tah-leech-kah) (kah-toh-leek)
3. **католичка / католик** _____
Catholic woman Catholic man

(moo-sool-mahn-kah) (moo-sool-mah-neen)
4. **мусульманка/мусульманин** _____
Moslem woman Moslem man

(tsair-kahv) *(vuh)*
Церковь в Москве. ⟶
church

(prah-vah-slahv-nah-yah) (tsair-kahv)
Это православная церковь?
is it Orthodox

(no-vah-yah) *(nyet) (stah-rah-yah)*
Это новая церковь? Нет, старая.
is it new no old

(mnoh-gah) (krah-see-vihk) (tsair-kvay)
You will see **много красивых церквей**
many pretty churches

(vuh)
like this during your holiday **в**

(es-es-es-air)
СССР.
U.S.S.R.

Теперь, let's learn how to say "I am" **по-русски**:
(pah-roos-skee)

(yah)
I am = **я** _____

(yah) (suh)
Practice saying „**я**" **с** the following **словами**. **Теперь** write each sentence for more practice.

Make sure you understand what you are saying.

(kah-tah-leech-kah)
Я католичка. _____
I am

(prah-vah-slahv-nah-yah)
Я православная. _____

(eev-ray)
Я еврей. _____

(ah-myeh-ree-kah-neets)
Я американец. _____
American

(vuh) (es-es-es-air)
Я в СССР. _____

(kah-nahd-yets)
Я канадец. _Я канадец._
Canadian

(ahv-strah-lee-yets)
Я австралиец. _____
Australian

(ahn-glee-chahn-kah)
Я англичанка. _____
English

☐ **дискуссия** *(dee-skoos-see-yah)* . . . . discussion _____
☐ **доктор** *(dohk-tar)* . . . . doctor _____
☐ **документ** *(dah-koo-myent)* . . . . document **Д** _____
☐ **доллар** *(dohl-lar)* . . . . dollar _____
☐ **драма** *(drah-mah)* . . . . drama _____

35

(yah) (vuh) (tsair-kvee)
Я в церкви. _____
I am in church

(yah) (koohk-nyeh)
Я в кухне. _____

(moo-sool-mah-neen)
Я мусульманин. _____

(eev-ray-kah)
Я еврейка. _____

(gah-stee-neet-seh)
Я в гостинице. _____
hotel

(res-tah-rahn-yeh)
Я в ресторане. _____
restaurant

(go-lah-dyen)
Я голоден. _____
hungry

(hah-choo) (peet)
Я хочу пить. _____
thirsty

Теперь identify all *(lood-yeh)* **людей** *(kar-teen-kyeh)* **на картинке** below by writing *(prah-veel-nah-yeh)* **правильное** *(roos-skah-yeh)* **русское слово** for
people   correct

each person on the line with the corresponding number *(pohd)* **под** *(kar-teen-koy)* **картинкои.**
under picture

1. _____   2. _____

3. _____   4. _____

5. _____   6. _____

7. Михаил Глебович   8. _____

9. _____   10. _____

Are **вы** ready for a Russian rhyme?

(et-tah) (kohl-yeh)   *(shkohl-yeh) (pyah-tahm) (klas-seh)*
Это Коля с братом Васей. Коля в Школе в пятом классе.
Kolya   (his) brother Vasya   school   fifth   class

☐ **жакет** *(zhah-kyet)* .... jacket (woman's) _____
☐ **жасмин** *(zhahs-meen)* .... jasmine _____
☐ **желе** *(zhyel-yeh)* .... jelly _____
☐ **журнал** *(zhoor-nahl)* .... journal, magazine **ж** _____
☐ **—журналист** *(zhoor-nah-leest)* .... journalist

(ee-zoo-chy-tee)
Изучайте!
learn

You have already used the verbs *(oo)(men-yah)* **у меня** *(yest)* **есть,** *(yah)* **я** *(hah-choo)* **хочу** and *(ee-dyoht)* **идёт.** Although you might
I have   I   would like   goes

be able to get by with these verbs, let's assume you want to do better. First a quick review.

How do you say ☐ **"I"** *(pah-roos-skee)* **по-русски?** _____ How do you say ☐ **"we"** **по-русски?** _____

Compare these *(dvah)* **два** charts
two
(oh-cheen) **очень** carefully **и** learn these
very
(shest) *(slohv)* **шесть слов** on the right.
six

I = *(yah)* **я**	we = *(mwee)* **мы**
he = *(ohn)* **он**	you = *(vwee)* **вы**
she = *(oh-nah)* **она**	they = *(oh-nee)* **они**

Not too hard, is it? **Теперь** draw lines between the matching English **и русские** *(roos-skee-yeh)* *(sloh-vah)* **слова**

below to see if you can keep these **слова** straight in your mind.

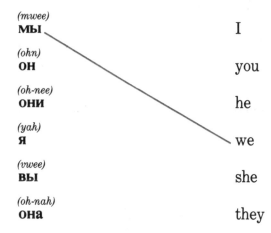

(mwee) **МЫ** — I

(ohn) **ОН** — you

(oh-nee) **ОНИ** — he

(yah) **Я** — we

(vwee) **ВЫ** — she

(oh-nah) **ОНА** — they

(teep-yair) **Теперь** close *(kuh-nee-goo)(ee)* **книгу и** write out both columns of the above practice on *(boo-mahg-yeh)* **бумаге.** How did
paper
(vwee) **вы** do? *(hah-rah-shoh)* **Хорошо** *(ploh-hah)* **или плохо?** *(hah-rah-shoh)* **Хорошо** **или** *(nyet)* **нет? Теперь** that *(vwee)* **вы** know these **слова,**
you   good   or   bad   good   not   you
(vwee) **вы** can say almost anything **по-русски** with one basic formula: the "plug-in" formula.
you
With this formula, *(vwee)* **вы** can correctly use any **слова вы** wish.
you

☐ **зона** *(zoh-nah)*	zone	_____
☐ **зоопарк** *(zah-oh-park)*	zoo	_____
☐ **импортный** *(eem-port-nee)*	imported	_____
☐ **Индия** *(een-dee-yah)*	India	_____
☐ **индустриальный** *(een-doo-stree-ahl-nee)*	industrial	_____

3

To demonstrate, let's take **шесть** *(shest)* basic **и** practical verbs **и** see how the "plug-in" formula works. Write the verbs in the blanks below after **вы** have practiced saying them out loud many times.

(zah-kah-zih-vaht)
заказывать = to order/reserve

заказывать

(pah-koo-paht)
покупать = to buy

_____

(ee-zoo-chaht)
изучать = to learn

_____

(pohv-tar-yaht)
повторять = to repeat

_____

(poh-nee-maht)
понимать = to understand

_____

(gah-vah-reet)
говорить = to speak

_____

Study the following patterns carefully.

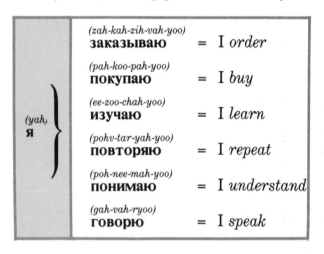

(yah, **я**

(zah-kah-zih-vah-yoo)
заказываю = I *order*

(pah-koo-pah-yoo)
покупаю = I *buy*

(ee-zoo-chah-yoo)
изучаю = I *learn*

(pohv-tar-yah-yoo)
повторяю = I *repeat*

(poh-nee-mah-yoo)
понимаю = I *understand*

(gah-vah-ryoo)
говорю = I *speak*

(ohn) **он**

(oh-nah) **она**

(zah-kah-zih-vah-yet)
заказывает = he/she *orders*

(pah-koo-pah-yet)
покупает = he/she *buys*

(ee-zoo-chah-yet)
изучает = he/she *learns*

(pohv-tar-yah-yet)
повторяет = he/she *repeats*

(poh-nee-mah-yet)
понимает = he/she *understands*

(gah-vah-reet)
говорит = he/she *speaks*

Note: • With all these verbs, the first thing you do is drop the final „**ть**" from the basic verb form.

• With **я**, you add **ю** *(yoo)* or **у** *(oo)* to the basic verb form. This is basically the sound "*oo*."

• With **он** or **она**, you add the sound "*yet*" (**ет**) to the basic verb form or the sound "*eet*" (**ит**).

Some verbs just will not conform to the pattern! But don't worry. Speak slowly **и** clearly, **и** you will be perfectly understood whether you say **изучаю** *(ee-zoo-chah-yoo)* or **изучает** *(ee-zoo-chah-yet)*. **Русские** Russians will be delighted that you have taken the time to learn their language.

☐ **инженер** *(een-zhen-yair)* . . . . engineer _____
☐ **инспектор** *(een-spyek-tar)* . . . . inspector _____
☐ **институт** *(een-stee-toot)* . . . . institute _____
☐ **инструктор** *(een-strook-tar)* . . . . instructor **И** _____

38 ☐ **инструмент** *(een-stroo-myent)* . . . . instrument _____

Here's your pattern for **мы** *(mwee)* _{we}. Add the sound "*eem*": **ем** or **им**.

мы	*(zah-kah-zih-vah-eem)* **заказываем**	= we *order*		**мы**	*(pohv-tar-yah-eem)* **повторяем**	= we *repeat*
	(pah-koo-pah-eem) **покупаем**	= we *buy*			*(poh-nee-mah-eem)* **понимаем**	= we *understand*
	(ee-zoo-chah-eem) **изучаем**	= we *learn*			*(gah-vah-reem)* **говорим**	= we *speak*

Here's your pattern for **вы** *(vwee)*. Add the sound "*yet-yeh*" (**ете**) or "*ee-tee*" (**ите**).

вы	*(zah-kah-zih-vah-yet-yeh)* **заказываете**	= you *order*		**вы**	*(pohv-tar-yah-yet-yeh)* **повторяете**	= you *repeat*
	(pah-koo-pah-yet-yeh) **покупаете**	= you *buy*			*(poh-nee-mah-yet-yeh)* **понимаете**	= you *understand*
	(ee-zoo-chah-yet-yeh) **изучаете**	you *learn*			*(gah-vah-ree-tee)* **говорите**	you *speak*

Finally, here's your pattern for **они**, *(oh-nee)* _{they} which calls for the sound "*yoot*" (**ют**) or sometimes

они	*(zah-kah-zih-vah-yoot)* **заказывают**	= they *order*		**они**	*(pohv-tar-yah-yoot)* **повторяют**	= they *repeat*
	(pah-koo-pah-yoot) **покупают**	= they *buy*			*(poh-nee-mah-yoot)* **понимают**	= they *understand*
	(ee-zoo-chah-yoot) **изучают**	= they *learn*			*(gah-var-yaht)* **говорят**	= they *speak*

Теперь it is your turn to practice **что вы** *(chtoh) (vwee)* _{what} have learned. Fill in the following blanks **с** the

correct form of the verb. Each time **вы** write out the sentence, be sure to say it aloud.

(zah-kah-zih-vaht)
заказывать
to order/reserve

(pah-koo-paht)
покупать
to buy

(yah)
Я _____ *(stah-kahn)* **стакан** *(voh-dih)* **воды.**
_{glass} _{water}

Я _____ *(kuh-nee-goo)* **книгу.**
_{book}

Он _____ **стакан** *(vee-nah)* **вина.**
Она

Он покупает **салат.**
Она

(mwee)
Мы _____ **стакан** *(mah-lah-kah)* **молока.**

Мы _____ *(lahm-poo)* **лампу.**

(vwee)
Вы заказываете *(chahsh-koo)* **чашку** *(chah-yah)* **чая.**
_{cup} _{tea}

Вы _____ *(chah-see)* **часы.**
_{clock}

(oh-nee)
Они _____ **чашку** *(kohf-yeh)* **кофе.**

Они _____ *(beel-yet)* **билет.**
_{ticket}

☐	**интеллигент** *(een-tyel-lee-gyent)*	intellectual	_____
☐	**интенрвю** *(een-tyair-view)*	interview	_____
☐	**интенес** *(een-tyair-yes)*	interest	**И**
☐	**интернациональный** *(een-tyair-naht-see-oh-nahl-nee)*	international	_____
☐	**информация** *(een-far-maht-see-yah)*	information	_____

(ee-zoo-chaht)
изучать
to learn

Я _____ **русский.**
(roos-skee)
Russian

Он _____ **русский.**
Она

Мы _____ **английский.**
(ahn-glee-skee)
English

Вы *изучаете* _____ **английский.**

Они _____ **немецкий.**
(nee-myet-skee)
German

(pohv-tar-yaht)
повторять
to repeat

Я _____ **слово.**
(yah) *(sloh-vah)*

Он _____ **ответы.**
Она
(aht-vyet-ee)
answers

Мы *повторяем* _____ **ответы.**

Вы _____ **число.**
(chee-slah)
number

Они _____ **вопросы.**
(vah-proh-see)
questions

(poh-nee-maht)
понимать
to understand

Я *понимаю* _____ **по-английски.**
(pah-ahn-glee-skee)

Он _____ **по-русски.**
Она

Мы _____ **по-немецки.**
(pah-nee-myet-skee)
German

Вы _____ **по-французски.**
(pah-frahn-tsoo-skee)
French

Они _____ **по-испански.**
(pah-ee-spahn-skee)
Spanish

(gah-vah-reet)
говорить
to speak/say

Я _____ **по-русски.**
(pah-roos-skee)
Russian

Он _____ **по-английски.**
Она

Мы _____ **по-итальянски.**
(pah-ee-tahl-yahn-skee)
Italian

Вы _____ **по-русски.**

Они *говорят* _____ **по-английски.**

(voht) *(shest)*
Вот шесть more verbs.
here are six

ехать = to go
(yek-haht) (by vehicle)

приезжать = to arrive
(pree-yez-zhaht)

видеть = to see
(vee-deet)

_____   _____   _____

жить = to live/reside
(zheet)

ждать = to wait for
(zhdaht)

искать = to look for
(ees-kaht)

жить _____   _____   _____

At the back of **книги,** **вы** will find **семь страниц** of flash cards to help you learn these
(kuh-nee-gee) *(syem)* *(strah-neets)*
pages

новые слова. Cut them out; carry them in your briefcase, purse, pocket **или** knapsack; **и**
(noh-vih-yeh)
new

review them whenever **вы** have a free moment.
(vwee)

Теперь fill in the following blanks with the correct form of each verb. Be sure to say each sentence out loud until **вы** have it down pat!
<small>you</small>

(yek-haht)
ехать
to go

Я _еду/_____ **в** **СССР.**
<small>to</small> <small>U.S.S.R.</small>
(vuh) (es-es-es-air)

Он _едет/_____ **в** **Москву.**
Она
(mahsk-voo)

Мы _едем/_____ **в** **Ленинград.**
<small>Leningrad</small>
(lee-neen-grahd)

Вы _едете/_____ **в** **гостиницу.**
<small>hotel</small>
(gah-stee-neet-soo)

Они _еду/т/_____ **в** **Горький.**
<small>Gorki</small>
(gor-kee)

(pree-yez-zhaht)
приезжать
to arrive

Я _приезжаю/_____ **из** **Москвы.**
<small>from</small>
(eez) (mahsk-vee)

Он _приезжает/_____ **из** **Канады.**
Она <small>Canada</small>
(eez) (kah-nah-dee)

Мы _приезжаем/_____ **из** **СССР.**
(eez) (es-es-es-air)

Вы _приезжаете/_____ **из** **Ленинграда.**
<small>Leningrad</small>
(lee-neen-grah-dah)

Они _приезжают/_____ **из** **Австралии.**
<small>Australia</small>
(ahv-strah-lee-ee)

(vee-deet)
видеть
to see

Я _вижу/_____ **гостиницу.**
<small>hotel</small>
(gah-stee-neet-soo)

Он _видит/_____ **такси.**
Она <small>taxi</small>
(tahk-see)

Мы _видим/_____ **ресторан.**
<small>restaurant</small>
(res-tah-rahn)

Вы _видите/_____ **банк.**
<small>bank</small>
(bahnk)

Они _видят/_____ **Москву.**
(mahsk-voo)

(zheet)
жить
to live/reside

Я _живу/_____ **в** **СССР.**
(vuh) (es-es-es-air)

Он _живёт/_____ **в Америке.**
Она <small>America</small>
(ah-myeh-ree-kyeh)

Мы _живём/_____ **в** **Канаде.**
<small>Canada</small>
(kah-nahd-yeh)

Вы _живёте/_____ **в** **Англии.**
<small>England</small>
(ahn-glee-ee)

Они _живут/_____ **в** **Австралии.**
<small>Australia</small>
(ahv-strah-lee-ee)

(zhdaht)
ждать
to wait for

Я _жду/_____ **такси.**
(tahk-see)

Он _ждёт/_____ **автобуса.**
Она <small>bus</small>
(ahv-toh-boo-sah)

Мы _ждём/_____ **Ивана.**
<small>Ivan</small>
(ee-vah-nah)

Вы _ждёте/_____ **Анну.**
<small>Anna</small>
(ahn-noo)

Они _ждут/_____ **меню.**
<small>menu</small>
(myen-yoo)

(ees-kaht)
искать
to look for

Я _ищу/_____ **марку.**
<small>stamp</small>
(mar-koo)

Он _ищет/_____ **цветы.**
Она <small>flowers</small>
(tsvet-ee)

Мы _ищем/_____ **туалет.**
(too-ahl-yet)

Вы _ищете/_____ **дом.**
<small>house</small>
(dohm)

Они _ищут/_____ **книгу.**
<small>book</small>
(kuh-nee-goo)

☐ **камера** *(kah-myair-ah)* . . . . camera
☐ **Канада** *(kah-nah-dah)* . . . . Canada
☐ **канал** *(kah-nahl)* . . . . canal
☐ **канарейка** *(kah-nah-ray-kah)* . . . . canary
☐ **кандидат** *(kahn-dee-daht)* . . . . candidate

к _____

_____

41

Теперь take a deep breath. See if **вы** *(vwee)* can fill in the blanks below. The correct **ответы** are

at the bottom of **этой** *(et-toy)* **страницы.**
this

1. I speak Russian. _____

2. He arrives from America. _____

3. We learn Russian. _____

4. They repeat the number._____

5. She understands English. _____

6. We go to the U.S.S.R. _Мы едем в СССР._

7. I see the hotel. _____

8. I live in Canada. _____

9. You buy a book._____

10. He orders a glass of water. _____

Да, *(dah)* it is hard to get used to all those **новым словам.** *(noh-vim)* But just keep practicing **и,** *(ee)* before
yes   *new*

вы *(vwee)* know it, **вы** will be using them naturally.

In the following Steps, **вы** *(vwee)* will be introduced to more **и** more verbs **и вы** should drill them

in exactly the same way as **вы** *(vwee)* did in this section. Look up **новые слова** *(noh-vih-yeh)* in your **словаре** *(slah-var-yeh)* **и**
                                                                       new   *dictionary*

make up your own sentences using the same type of pattern. Try out your **новые слова** *(noh-vih-yeh)*
                                                                                       new

for that's how you make them yours to use on your holiday. Remember, the more **вы** *(vwee)*

practice **теперь,** *(teep-yair)* the more enjoyable your trip will be. **Удачи!** *(oo-dah-chee)*
                                                                          good luck

Теперь is a perfect time to turn to the back of this **книги,** *(kuh-nee-gee)* clip out your verb flash cards **и**

start flashing. Also, don't skip over your free **слова.** Be sure to check them off in the box

provided as **вы** **изучаете** *(ee-zoo-chah-yet-yeh)* each one.
                        learn

(skohl-kah) *(vreh-mee-nee)*
Сколько Времени?
what   time is it

(vwee)   *(kahk)*   *(dnee)* *(nee-dyel-ee)* *(myes-yet-see)* *(go-dah)*
Вы know **как** to tell **дни недели и месяцы года,** so now let's learn to tell time.
days of week   months   of year

              (vuh)   *(rez-yair-vaht-see-yoo)*
As a traveler **в СССР, вы** need to be able to tell time in order to make **резервацию и**
reservations

(poh-yez-dah)
to catch **поезда и автобусы.**   *(voht)* **Вот** the "basics."
     trains   buses   here are

o'clock/hour	=	*(chahs)* **час** _____
minutes	=	*(mee-noot)* **минут** _____
half	=	*(pah-lah-vee-nah)* **половина** _____
minus	=	*(byez)* **без** *без, без, без* _____

What time is it?	=	*(vreh-mee-nee)* **Сколько времени?**
		(kah-toh-ree) *(chahs)* **Который час?**
special endings	=	*(oh-vah)* **-ого**
		(yeh-vah) **-его**

(pree-myeh-rih) *(vnee-zoo)*
Теперь, как are these **слова** used? Study **примеры внизу.** When **вы** think it through, it
examples   below

      (nyeh)
really is **не** too difficult. Just notice that the pattern changes after the halfway mark.
not

(chah-sohv)
Пять часов.
o'clock

(dyes-yet) *(mee-noot)* *(shest-oh-vah)*
Десять минут шестого. = 5:10
ten   minutes (toward) sixth hour

(dvahd-tset) *(mee-noot)* *(shest-oh-vah)*
Двадцать минут шестого. = 5:20
twenty minutes (toward)sixth hour

(pah-lah-vee-nah)
Половина шестого. = 5:30
half (of)   sixth hour

(byez) *(dvahd-tset-ee)* *(shest)*
Без двадцати шесть. = 5:40
minus twenty (from) six

(dyes-yet-ee)
Без десяти шесть. = 5:50
ten (from)

(chah-sohv)
Шесть часов.

(syem) *(chah-sohv)*
Семь часов.

(dvahd-tset) *(vohs-moh-vah)*
Двадцать минут восьмого.
twenty   minutes (toward) eighth hour

(pah-lah-vee-nah) *(vohs-moh-vah)*
Половина восьмого.
half (of)   eighth hour

(byez) *(dvahd-tset-ee)* *(voh-syem)*
Без двадцати восемь.
twenty (from)   eight

(chah-sohv)
Восемь часов.

(vreh-myah)
Теперь fill in the blanks according to **время** indicated on **часах. Который час?**
time   clocks
(chah-sahk) *(kah-toh-ree)* *(chahs)*

1. _____

2. *Семь часов.* _____

3. _____

4. _____

ОТВЕТЫ

3. Половина восьмого.	4. Четыре часа.
1. Восемь часов.	2. Семь часов.

Вот more time-telling **слова** to add to your vocabulary.

(chet-virt)
четверть = a quarter (toward)

(byez) (chet-virt-ee)
без четверти = minus a quarter (from)

(byez) (chet-virt-ee)
Без четверти два.
minus a quarter (from)   two

(dyev-yet)
Без четверти девять.
nine

(chet-virt)   (vtah-roh-vah)
Четверть второго.
a quarter (toward)   two

(dyes-yaht-oh-vah)
Четверть десятого.

(kah-toh-ree)   (chahs)
Теперь, it is your turn. **Который час?**

Четверть шестого .
четверть шестого

_____ .
без четверти семь

_____ .
без четверти три

_____ .
четверть седьмого

(chee-slah)
See how **важно** learning **числа** is? **Теперь** answer the following **вопросы** based on **часах**
important   numbers   *(vah-proh-see)*   *(chah-sahk)*
                                                                              questions   clocks

below. **Ответы** are at the bottom of **страницы.**

(skohl-kah)   (vreh-mee-nee)
Сколько времени?

1. _____

2. _____

3. Восемь часов. _____

4. _____

5. _____

6. _____

7. _____

When **вы** *(vwee)* answer a „**когда**" *(kahg-dah)* question, say „**в**" *(vuh)* before **вы** *(vwee)* give the time.
                                                                          when   at

Когда **придёт** **поезд?** *(pree-dyoht)* *(poh-yezd)* В ШЕСТЬ ЧАСОВ.
         comes   train

поезд
43 **6:00**

Теперь answer the following **вопросы** *(vah-proh-see)* based on **часах** *(chah-sahk)* **внизу** *(vnee-zoo)*. Be sure to practice saying
                             questions   clocks   below

each **вопрос** *(vah-prohs)* out loud several times.
     question

Когда **начинается** **концерт?** *(kahg-dah)* *(nah-chee-nah-yet-syah)* *(kohn-tsairt)* _____
         begins   concert

Когда **начинается** **фильм?** *(nah-chee-nah-yet-syah)* *(feelm)* В СЕМЬ ЧАСОВ _____
         begins   film

Когда **придёт** **автобус?** *(kahg-dah)* *(pree-dyoht)* *(ahv-toh-boos)* _____
         comes   bus

Когда **придёт** **такси?** *(pree-dyoht)* *(tahk-see)* _____
         comes

Когда **открывается** **ресторан?** *(aht-krih-vah-yet-syah)* *(res-tah-rahn)* _____
         opens   restaurant

Когда **закрывается** **ресторан?** *(zah-krih-vah-yet-syah)*
         closes

В **восемь часов утра, мы** *(vuh)* *(voh-syem)* *(oo-trah)*
at   in morning
говорим „**Доброе** **утро,** *(gah-vah-reem)* *(doh-brah-yeh)* *(oo-trah)*
say   good   morning
Мария Николаевна." *(nee-koh-lah-eev-nah)*

В **восемь часов** **вечера, мы** *(chah-sohv)* *(vyeh-cheh-rah)*
                     in evening
говорим „**Добрый** **вечер,** *(doh-brih)* *(vyeh-cher)*

Анна Петровна." *(pee-trohv-nah)*

В **час** **дня, мы говорим** *(chahs)* *(den-yah)* *(mwee)*
one   in afternoon
„**Добрый** **день,** *(dyen)*
Иван Николаевич." *(nee-koh-lah-ee-veech)*

В **десять часов вечера, мы** *(dyes-yet)*
ten   in evening
говорим „**Спокойной** **ночи,** *(spah-koy-noy)* *(noh-chee)*
          good   night
Зина Ивановна." *(ee-vah-nohv-nah)*

45

Remember:

| What time is it? | = | *(kah-toh-ree)*
Который час?
(vreh-mee-nee)
Сколько времени? |

| When | = | **Когда** |

(vwee)
Can **вы** pronounce **и** understand the

following paragraph?

(poh-yezd) (eez)   *(pree-dyoht)*   *(chet-virt)*
Поезд из Москвы придёт в четверть
train   from
(shest-oh-vah)   *(dvahd-tset)*
шестого. Теперь двадцать минут шестого.

(ah-pahz-dahl)   *(see-vohd-nyah)*   *(pree-dyoht)*
Поезд опоздал. Сегодня поезд придёт
late   today
(vohs-moh-vah)   *(zahv-trah)*   *(pree-dyoht)*
в четверть восьмого. Завтра поезд придёт
tomorrow

в четверть шестого.

(voht)
Вот some more practice exercises. Answer **вопросы** *(vah-proh-see)* based on the times given below.

(kah-toh-ree)   *(chahs)*
Который час?

1. (10:30) _____

2. (6:30) Половина седьмого.

3. (6:15) _____

4. (10:45) _____

5. (5:45) _____

6. (7:20) _____

7. (3:10) _____

8. (4:05) _____

9. (8:30) _____

10. (4:00) _____

☐ **клоун** *(kloh-oon)* . . . . clown
☐ **коллекция** *(kahl-yekt-see-yah)* . . . . collection
☐ **командир** *(kah-mahn-deer)* . . . . commander
☐ **комедия** *(kah-myeh-dee-yah)* . . . . comedy
☐ **комиссар** *(kah-mees-sar)* . . . . commissar

к

(voht) **Вот** a quick quiz. Fill in the blanks *(suh)* **с** the correct *(chee-slah-mee)* **числами.** *(aht-vyet-ee)* **Ответы** *(vnee-zoo)* **внизу.**

numbers   below

1. **В** *(vuh)* *(mee-noot-yeh)* **минуте** _____ **секунд.** *(see-koond)*

   minute (there are)   (?)   seconds

5. **В году** *(gah-doo)* _____ **месяцев.** *(myes-yet-syev)*

   months

2. **В** *(chahs-yeh)* **часе** _____ **минут.**

   hour   (?)   minutes

6. **В году** *(nee-dyel-ee)* _____ **недели.**

   weeks

3. **В** *(nee-dyel-yeh)* **неделе** *семь* _____ **дней.** *(dnay)*

   (?)   days

7. **В году** _____ **дней.**

   (?)

4. **В** *(myes-yets-yeh)* **месяце** _____ **дней.**

   (?)   days

8. **В феврале** _____ **дней.**

   (?)

If **вы** are traveling between large cities **в Советском Союзе, вы** will more than likely take

(poh-yezd) **поезд. Вы** may want to do as the *(roos-skee-yeh)* **русские** do **и** carry your luggage on the train, rather

train   Russians

than check it on board.

(voht) **Вот** a sample **страницы** *(eez)* **из** *(roos-skah-vah)* **русского** *(rah-spee-sah-nee-yah)* **расписания** *(poh-yez-dohv)* **поездов.**

from   schedule   of trains

Ленинград - Москва		
(aht-hah-deet) **Отходит** departs	**Поезд No.**	*(pree-dyoht)* **Придёт** arrives
0:41	50	12:41
7:40	19	19:40
12:15	10	0:15
14:32	4	2:32
21:40	22	9:40

ОТВЕТЫ

1. шестьдесят   2. шестьдесят   3. семь   4. тридцать   5. двенадцать   6. пятьдесят две   7. триста шестьдесят пять   8. двадцать восемь

47

(noh-vih-yeh)
Вот новые verbs for Step 12.
new

(gah-vah-reet)
говорить = to say/speak

(yest)
есть = to eat

(peet)
пить = to drink

_____   еСТЬ   _____

(gah-vah-reet)
говорить
to say

Я _____ „доброе утро.“
(doh-brah-yeh)

Он _____ „добрый день.“
Она   *(doh-brih)* *(dyen)*

Мы   ГОВОРИМ   „нет.“
(nyet)
no

Вы _____ „да.“
(dah)
yes

(oh-nee)
Они _____ „Спасибо.“
(spah-see-bah)

(yest)
есть
to eat

(yah)
Я ем/ _____ суп.
(soop)

Он ест/ _____ борщ.
Она   *(borsht)*

Мы едим/ _____ много.
(mnoh-gah)
a lot

Вы едите/ _____ хлеб.
(hlyeb)
bread

Они едят/ _____ рыбу.
(rib-oo)
fish

(peet)
пить
to drink

Я пью/ _____ молоко.
milk

Он пьёт/ _____ белое вино.
Она   *(byel-lah-yeh)* *(vee-noh)*
                white

(mwee)
Мы пьём/ _____ пиво.
(pee-vah)

Вы пьёте/ _____ стакан воды.
(stah-kahn) *(voh-dih)*

Они пьют/ _____ чай.
(chy)
tea

As **вы** have probably noticed, the sound of the Russian letter „й“ varies greatly. Here are

some examples.

(kar-teen-koy)	*(eev-ray-kah)*	*(moo-zay)*	*(chy)*	*(syeh-ree)*
картинкой	**еврейка**	**музей**	**чай**	**серый**
picture	Jewish woman	museum	tea	blue

☐ **коммунист** *(kahm-moo-neest)*............	communist	_____
☐ **компас** *(kohm-pahs)*......................	compass	_____
☐ **композитор** *(kahm-pah-zee-tar)*..........	composer	**К** _____
☐ **конференция** *(kahn-fyair-yent-see-yah)*......	conference	_____
☐ **концерт** *(kohn-tsairt)*....................	concert	_____

48

(kar-tee-nah) **картина**	*(gah-stee-nah-yah)* **ГОСТИНАЯ**	*(dyev-yet)* **9 девять**	*(doh-brih)* *(dyen)* **добрый день**
(pah-tah-lohk) **ПОТОЛОК**	*(gah-rahzh)* **гараж**	*(dyes-yet)* **10 десять**	*(doh-brih)* *(vyeh-cher)* **добрый вечер**
(oog-ahl) **УГОЛ**	*(pahd-vahl)* **ПОДВАЛ**	*(chyor-nee)* **чёрный**	*(spah-koy-nih)* *(noh-chee)* **спокойной ночи**
(ahk-noh) **окно**	*(ahv-tah-mah-beel)* **автомобиль**	*(zhyol-tee)* **жёлтый**	*(kahk)* *(dee-lah)* **Как дела?**
(lahm-pah) **лампа**	*(moh-tah-tsee-kul)* **МОТОЦИКЛ**	*(see-nee)* **синий**	*(hah-lah-deel-neek)* **холодильник**
(dee-vahn) **диван**	*(sah-bah-kah)* **собака**	*(syeh-ree)* **серый**	*(plee-tah)* **плита**
(stool) **стул**	*(koht)* **кот**	*(kah-reech-nyeh-vwee)* **коричневый**	*(vee-noh)* **вино**
(kahv-yor) **ковёр**	*(sahd)* **сад**	*(roh-zah-vwee)* **розовый**	*(pee-vah)* **пиво**
(stohl) **стол**	*(poach-tah)* **почта**	*(byel-lee)* **белый**	*(mah-lah-koh)* **молоко**
(dvyair) **дверь**	*(putch-toh-vee)* *(yahsh-chik)* **почтовый ящик**	*(krahs-nee)* **красный**	*(mah-slah)* **масло**
(chah-see) **часы**	*(tsvet-ee)* **цветы**	*(zyel-yoh-nee)* **зелёный**	*(tar-yel-kah)* **тарелка**
(zah-nahv-yes) **занавес**	*(zvah-nohk)* **звонок**	*(oh-rahn-zheh-vwee)* **оранжевый**	*(sole)* **соль**
(styen-ah) **стена**	*(ah-deen)* **1 один**	*(pah-nee-dyel-neek)* **понедельник**	*(pyeh-reets)* **перец**
(teh-leh-fohn) **телефон**	*(dvah)* **2 два**	*(vtor-neek)* **вторник**	*(nohzh)* **нож**
(dohm) **дом**	*(tree)* **3 три**	*(sree-dah)* **среда**	*(chahsh-kah)* **чашка**
(kah-bee-nyet) **кабинет**	*(cheh-tir-ee)* **4 четыре**	*(chet-vyairg)* **четверг**	*(veel-kah)* **вилка**
(vahn-nah-yah) **ванная**	*(pyaht)* **5 пять**	*(pyaht-neet-sah)* **пятница**	*(stah-kahn)* **стакан**
(koohk-nyah) **кухня**	*(shest)* **6 шесть**	*(soo-boh-tah)* **суббота**	*(sahl-fyet-kah)* **салфетка**
(spahl-nyah) **спальня**	*(syem)* **7 семь**	*(voh-skree-syen-yah)* **воскресенье**	*(lohzh-kah)* **ложка**
(stah-loh-vah-yah) **столовая**	*(voh-syem)* **8 восемь**	*(doh-brah-yeh)* *(oo-trah)* **доброе утро**	*(shkahf)* **шкаф**

STICKY LABELS

This book has over 150 special sticky labels for you to use as you learn new words. When you are introduced to a word, remove the corresponding label from these pages. Be sure to use each of these unique labels by adhering them to a picture, window, lamp, or whatever object it refers to. The sticky labels make learning to speak Russian much more fun and a lot easier than you ever expected.

For example, when you look in the mirror and see the label, say

(zyair-kah-lah)
,,зеркало.“ ”

Don't just say it once, say it again and again.

And once you label the refrigerator, you should never again open that door without saying

(hah-lah-deel-neek)
,,холодильник.“

By using the sticky labels, you not only learn new words but friends and family learn along with you!

(hlyeb) **хлеб**	*(zhoor-nahl)* **журнал**	*(gryeb-yen)* **гребень**	*(roo-bahsh-kah)* **рубашка**
(chy) **чай**	*(gah-zyet-ah)* **газета**	*(pahl-toh)* **пальто**	*(peed-zhahk)* **пиджак**
(kohf-yeh) **кофе**	*(ahch-kee)* **очки**	*(plahshch)* **плащ**	*(bryoo-kee)* **брюки**
(krah-vaht) **кровать**	*(tee-lee-vee-zar)* **телевизор**	*(zohn-teek)* **зонтик**	*(plaht-yeh)* **платье**
(ah-dee-yah-lah) **одеяло**	*(kar-zee-nah)* **корзина**	*(pyair-chaht-kee)* **перчатки**	*(blooz-kah)* **блузка**
(pah-doosh-kah) **подушка**	*(pahs-port)* **паспорт**	*(shil-yah-pah)* **шляпа**	*(yoob-kah)* **юбка**
(boo-deel-neek) **будильник**	*(beel-yet)* **билет**	*(sah-poh-gee)* **сапоги**	*(sveet-yair)* **свитер**
(shkahf) **шкаф**	*(cheh-mah-dahn)* **чемодан**	*(too-flee)* **туфли**	*(leef-cheek)* **лифчик**
(oo-mih-vahl-neek) **умывальник**	*(soom-kah)* **сумка**	*(nah-skee)* **носки**	*(kohm-bee-naht-see-yah)* **комбинация**
(doosh) **душ**	*(boo-mahzh-neek)* **бумажник**	*(chool-kee)* **чулки**	*(troo-sih)* **трусы**
(too-ahl-yet) **туалет**	*(dyen-gee)* **деньги**	*(pee-zhah-mah)* **пижама**	*(may-kah)* **майка**
(zyair-kah-lah) **зеркало**	*(foh-toh-ahp-pah-raht)* **фотоаппарат**	*(nohch-nah-yah)* **ночная** *(roo-bahsh-kah)* **рубашка**	*(zahn-yah-tah)* **занято**
(pahl-ah-tyent-sah) **полотенца**	*(feelm)* **фильм**	*(koo-pahl-nee)* **купальный** *(hah-laht)* **халат**	*(eez-vee-nee-tee)* **извините**
(kah-rahn-dahsh) **карандаш**	*(koo-pahl-nee)* **купальный** *(kohst-yoom)* **костюм**	*(bahsh-mah-kee)* **башмаки**	*(aht-krit-tah)* **открыто**
(rooch-kah) **пучка**	*(sahn-dahl-ee)* **сандали**	*(kohst-yoom)* **костюм**	*(pree-yaht-nah-vah)* **приятного** *(ahp-pyeh-tee-tah)* **аппетита**
(boo-mah-gah) **бумага**	*(mwee-lah)* **мыло**	*(gahl-stook)* **галстук**	*(zah-krit-tah)* **закрыто**
(pees-moh) **письмо**	*(zoob-nah-yah)* **зубная** *(shyoht-kah)* **щётка**	*(plah-tohk)* **платок**	*(voh-dah)* **вода**
(aht-krit-kah) **открытка**	*(zoob-nah-yah)* **зубная** *(pahs-tah)* **паста**	*(yah)* **Я** *(ah-myeh-ree-kah-neets)* **американец.**	
(mar-kah) **марка**	*(breet-vah)* **бритва**	*(yah)* **Я** *(hah-choo)* **хочу** *(ee-zoo-chaht)* **изучать** *(roos-skee)* **русский.**	
(kuh-nee-gah) **книга**	*(dyeh-zah-doh-rahnt)* **дезодорант**	*(men-yah)* **Меня** *(zah-voot)* **зовут** _____ .	

PLUS . . .

Your book includes a number of other innovative features. At the back of the book, you'll find seven pages of flash cards. Cut them out and flip through them at least once a day.

On pages 112 and 113, you'll find a beverage guide and a menu guide. Don't wait until your trip to use them. Clip out the menu guide and use it tonight at the dinner table. And use the beverage guide to practice ordering your favorite drinks.

By using the special features in this book, you will be speaking Russian before you know it.

(oo-dah-chee)
Удачи!
good luck

(syev-eer)	*(yoog)*	*(vah-stohk)*	*(zah-pahd)*
Север -	**Юг,**	**Восток** -	**Запад**
north	south	east	west

(vwee)   *(kar-too)*   *(nyeh)*
If **вы** are looking at **карту** **и** **вы** see the following **слова**, it should **не** be too difficult to

map
(chtoh) *(oh-nee)*   *(vnee-zoo)*
figure out **что** **они** mean. Take an educated guess. **Ответы внизу.**

what   they   below

(syev-eer-nah-yah) *(dah-koh-tah)*	*(yoozh-nah-yah)*	*(zah-pahd-nee)* *(bair-leen)*
Северная Дакота	**Южная Дакота**	**Западный Берлин**
(ah-myeh-ree-kah)		*(zah-pahd-nah-yah)* *(gair-mah-nee-yah)*
Северная Америка	**Южная Америка**	**Западная Германия**
(kah-roh-lee-nah)		*(vah-stohch-nee)*
Северная Каролина	**Южная Каролина**	**Восточный Берлин**
(koh-reh-yah)	*(ah-free-kah)*	*(vah-stohch-nah-yah)*
Северная Корея	**Южная Африка**	**Восточная Германия**

(sloh-vah)   *(vlah-dee-vah-stohk)*
Do **вы** recognize **русское слово** for east in „**Владивосток**"? It means "eastern domain."

(vlah-dee-vah-stohk)   *(es-es-es-air)*
Владивосток is the easternmost seaport in **СССР.** It is also the terminus of the

(mahsk-vee)
Trans-Siberian Railroad, 5700 miles west of **Москвы.**

Moscow

(syev-eer)				*(syev-eer-nee)*		
север	= the north	_____		**северный**	= northern	_____
(yoog)				*(yoozh-nee)*		
юг	= the south	_____		**южный**	= southern	ЮЖНЫЙ
(vah-stohk)				*(vah-stohch-nee)*		
восток	= the east	ВОСТОК		**восточный**	= eastern	_____
(zah-pahd)				*(zah-pahd-nee)*		
запад	= the west	_____		**западный**	= western	_____

(oo-kah-zah-nee-yah)
But what about more basic **указания** such as "left," "right," **и** "straight ahead"?

directions

Let's learn these **слова.**

		(nah-lyev-ah)
to the left	=	**налево**
		(nah-prah-vah)
to the right	=	**направо**
		(pryah-mah)
straight ahead	=	**прямо**
		(nah) *(oo-gloo)*
on the corner	=	**на углу**

Just as **по-английски,** these **четыре** *(cheh-tir-ee)* **слова** go a long way.

in English   *four*

(pah-zhahl-yes-tah) **пожалуйста**	= please	_____
(spah-see-bah) **спасибо**	= thank you	*спасибо, спасибо, спасибо*
(eez-vee-nee-tee) **извините**	= excuse me	_____
(pah-zhahl-yes-tah) **пожалуйста**	= you're welcome	_____

(voht) *(dvah)*   *(dee-ah-loh-gah)*   *(dil-yah)*
Вот два typical **диалога** **для** someone who is trying to find something.

two   *dialogues/conversations*   *for*

(bor-ees) **Борис:**   *(eez-vee-nee-tee)* **Извините.** **Где** *(gah-stee-neet-sah)(lee-neen-grahd)* **гостиница Ленинград?**

excuse me   *hotel*   *Leningrad*

(lyen-ah) **Лена:**   *(prah-ee-dyoht-yeh)* **Пройдёте** *(doh)* **до** *(oo-leet-see)* **улицы** *(gairt-sen-ah)* **Герцена** **и** **там** *(nah-prah-vah)* **направо.**

go   *to*   *street*   *there*   *to the right*

(gah-stee-neet-sah) **Гостиница** *(lee-neen-grahd)* **Ленинград** *(nah)* **на** *(oo-gloo)* **углу.**

on   *corner*

(ohl-yeg) **Олег:**   *(eez-vee-nee-tee)* **Извините.** **Где** *(moo-zay)* **Музей** *(tohl-stoh-vah)* **Толстого?**

excuse me   *museum*   *Tolstoy*

(ohl-gah) **Ольга:**   *(prah-ee-dyoht-yeh)* **Пройдёте** *(nah-prah-vah)* **направо;** *(pah-tohm)* **потом** *(pryah-mah)* **прямо** *(doh)* **до** *(oo-leet-see)* **улицы**

go   *to the right*   *then*   *straight ahead*   *to*   *street*

(tohl-stoh-vah) **Толстого.** **Там** *(nah-lyev-ah)* **налево,** **и** *(moo-zay)* **музей** *(nah)* **на** *(oo-gloo)* **углу.**

Tolstoy   *to the left*

Are **вы** lost? There is no need to be lost if **вы** *(vwee)* have learned the basic direction **слова.**

Do not try to memorize these **диалоги** *(dee-ah-loh-gee)* because **вы** will never be looking for precisely

dialogues/conversations

these places. One day, **вы** might need to ask **указание** *(oo-kah-zah-nee-yeh)* to the **Большой Театр, ГУМ**

directions   *Bolshoi*   *Theater*   *GUM Department Store*

or **Кремль.** *(krem-il)* Learn the key direction **слова и** be sure **вы** can find your destination.

Kremlin

Вы may want to buy a guidebook to start planning what places **вы** would like to visit.

Practice asking **указания** *(oo-kah-zah-nee-yah)* to these special places. What if the person responding to your

directions

вопрос *(vah-prohs)* answers too quickly for **вы** to understand the entire reply? Look at the reply on

the next **странице.** Practice saying…

☐ **коньяк** *(kohn-yahk)*.................	cognac	_____
☐ **корт** *(kort)*..................	court (tennis)	_____
☐ **кот** *(koht)*..................	cat	_____
☐ **краб** *(krahb)*..................	crab	**К** _____
☐ **Куба** *(koo-bah)*..................	Cuba	_____

| | *(yah)* | *(nyeh)* | *(poh-nee-mah-yoo)* | *(pah-zhahl-yes-tah)* | *(pohv-tah-reet-yeh)* | *(spah-see-bah)* |

Извините. **Я** **не** **понимаю.** **Пожалуйста** **повторите.** **Спасибо.**
excuse me · I · (do) not understand · please · repeat

Теперь say it again **и** again.

Извините. Я не понимаю. Пожалуйста повторите. Спасибо.

(dah)
Да, it is difficult at first but don't give up! *(kahg-dah)* *(oo-kah-zah-nee-yah)* **Когда** **указания** are repeated, **вы** will be
yes · when · directions

able to understand if **вы** have learned the key **слова** for **указания.** *(oo-kah-zah-nee-yah)* Quiz yourself by filling

in the blanks below *(suh)* **с** the correct **русскими** *(roos-skee-mee)* *(slah-vah-mee)* **словами.**
words

	(ee-vahn) *(eez-vee-nee-tee)* *(res-tah-rahn)* *(sahd-koh)*
Иван:	**Извините. Где ресторан Садко?** restaurant

Таня: **Пройдёте**_____ *(oo)* *(mooz-yah)* **и у музея, пройдёте**
go · straight ahead · at

_____НАПРАВО_____. *(oo)* *(gah-stee-neet-see)* *(kohs-mohs)* **У гостиницы Космос пройдёте**
to the right · by · hotel

_____. *(sahd-koh)* **Ресторан Садко**_____. *(oo-dah-chee)* **Удачи!**
to the left · on the corner · good luck

(cheh-tir-ee) *(noh-vihk)* *(oh-nee)*
Вот четыре **новых** verbs. **Они** are different from the patterns **вы** have learned, so pay
new · they

close attention. **Вы** will probably use these verbs more than any others.

(yah)(hah-choo)
я **хочу** = I would like _____

(men-yeh) *(noozh-nah)*
мне **нужно** = I need . МНе НУЖНО _____

(men-yah) *(zah-voot)*
меня **зовут** = my name is... _____

(oo) *(men-yah)* *(yest)*
у меня **есть** = I have _____

☐ **лаборатория** *(lah-bah-rah-toh-ree-yah)* ...... laboratory _____
☐ **лимон** *(lee-mohn)* .... lemon _____
☐ **—лимонад** *(lee-moh-nahd)* .... lemonade **Л** _____
☐ **линия** *(lee-nee-yah)* .... line _____
☐ **литература** *(lee-tee-rah-too-rah)* .... literature _____

51

As always, say each sentence out loud. Say each **и** every **слово** carefully, pronouncing each **русский** sound as well as **вы** can.

(yah) (hah-choo)
Я   ХОЧУ
I   would like

Я _хочу/_ *(stah-kahn) (vee-nah)* стакан вина.
glass of

Он _хочет/_ *(mah-lah-kah)* стакан молока.
Она

(mwee)
Мы _ХОТИМ/_ *(voh-dih)* стакан воды.

Вы _хотите/_ *(chahsh-koo) (kohf-yeh)* чашку кофе.
cup of

Они _ХОТЯТ/_ *(chah-yah)* чашку чая.
they

(men-yah) (zah-voot)
МЕНЯ   ЗОВУТ…
my name is

(men-yah)
Меня _ЗОВУТ/_ *(nah-tahl-yah)* Наталья.

(yee-voh)
Его _____ Олег/Ольга.
(ee-yoh)
Её
Нас _ЗОВУТ/_ *(bor-ees) (lyen-ah)* Борис и Лена.
our name is

(vahs)
Вас _____ *(ahn-tohn)* Антон.
your name is

(eehk)
Их _ЗОВУТ/_ *(ahn-nah) (pyoh-ter)* Анна и Пётр.
their name is

(men-yeh) (noozh-nah)
МНЕ   НУЖНО
I   need

Мне _НУЖНО/_ *(stah-kahn) (lee-moh-nah-dah)* стакан лимонада.

(ee-moo)
Ему _____ стакан молока.
(yay)
Ей
Нам _НУЖНО/_ *(chahsh-koo)* чашку кофе.

(vahm)
Вам _____ *(chah-yah)* чашку чая.

(eem)
Им _НУЖНО/_ *(kah-kah-oh)* чашку какао.
cocoa

(oo) (men-yah) (yest)
у   меня   есть
I have

(oo) (men-yah)
У меня _____ *(pyaht) (kah-pyeh-eek)* пять копеек.

У него _есть/_ *(shest) (roo-blay)* шесть рублей.
(nyeh-voh)
(nyeh-yoh)
У неё
У нас _____ *(dyes-yet)* десять рублей.

(vahs)
У вас _есть/_ *(dveh) (kah-pay-kee)* две копейки.

(neehk)
У них _____ *(tree) (roob-lyah)* три рубля.

(teep-yair)
Теперь see if **вы** can translate the following thoughts **на русский**. *(aht-vyet-ee)* **Ответы** *(vnee-zoo)* **внизу**.
below

1. My name is …. _____

2. We would like a cup of coffee._____

3. I have six rubles. _У меня есть шесть рублей._

4. We need to buy a glass of lemonade._____

5. I need a cup of tea._____

6. We have five rubles._____

52

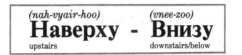
(nah-vyair-hoo) *(vnee-zoo)*

Наверху - Внизу

upstairs   downstairs/below

Before **вы** begin Step 14, review Step 8. *(teep-yair)* **Теперь** let's learn *(bohl-shee)* **больше слов.**
more

(dohm) *(vuh)* *(kee-yev-yeh)*
Дом в Киеве.
Kiev

(spahl-nyah) *(nah-vyair-hoo)*
Спальня наверху.
bedroom   (is) upstairs

(vahn-nah-yah) *(toh-zheh)* *(nah-vyair-hoo)*
Ванная тоже наверху.
bathroom   also

(gah-stee-nah-yah) *(vnee-zoo)*
Гостиная внизу.
living room   downstairs

(kah-bee-nyet) *(toh-zheh)* *(vnee-zoo)*
Кабинет тоже внизу.
study   also   downstairs

(teep-yair) **Теперь** go to your *(spahl-nyoo)* **спальню и** look around the *(kohm-nah-tee)* **комнаты.** Let's learn the names of the things
bedroom   room

(spahl-nyeh) **в спальне,** just like *(mwee)* **мы** learned the various parts of *(doh-mah)* **дома.** Be sure to practice saying
bedroom

all **слова** as **вы** write them in the spaces *(vnee-zoo)* **внизу.** Also say out loud the example sentences
below

(pohd) *(kar-teen-kah-mee)*
под картинками.
under   pictures

(krah-vaht)
кровать
bed

(ah-dee-yah-lah)
одеяло
blanket

(pah-doosh-kah)
подушка
pillow

Кровать большая.

(krah-vaht) *(bahl-shah-yah)*
Кровать большая.
bed   (is) big

(men-yeh) *(noozh-nah)* *(ah-dee-yah-lah)*
Мне нужно одеяло.
I   need

(men-yeh) *(noozh-nah)* *(pah-doosh-koo)*
Мне нужно подушку.
I   need

☐ **май** *(my)* .... May	
☐ **март** *(mart)* .... March	
☐ **масса** *(mahs-sah)* .... mass	**M**
☐ **мастер** *(mahs-tyair)* .... master	
☐ **математика** *(mah-tyeh-mah-tee-kah)* .... mathematics	

(boo-deel-neek)
будильник
alarm clock

(shkahf)
шкаф
wardrobe

Теперь, remove the next **пять** *(pyaht)*

stickers **и** label these things

(vuh) *(spahl-nyeh)*
в your **спальне.**

_____
(oo) *(men-yah)* *(yest)*
У меня есть
I have
(boo-deel-neek)
будильник.

_____
(vuh)(spahl-nyeh)
Шкаф в спальне.
bedroom

(spahl-nyah) *(gah-stee-neet-seh)*
Спальня в гостинице
hotel
(spaht)
спать = to sleep, so a sleeping room

Study the following **вопросы** **и** their *(vah-proh-see)*
questions
(aht-vyet-ee) *(nah)* *(kar-teen-kyeh)*
ответы based **на картинке** to the left.
on picture

1. *(gdyeh)* *(boo-deel-neek)*
Где будильник?
alarm clock

(boo-deel-neek) *(nah)* *(stohl-yeh)*
Будильник на столе.
on table

2. **Где одеяло?** *(ah-dee-yah-lah)*
blanket

(ah-dee-yah-lah) *(nah)* *(krah-vah-tee)*
Одеяло на кровати.
bed

3. **Где шкаф?** *(shkahf)*

(shkahf) *(vuh)* *(spahl-nyeh)*
Шкаф в спальне.
bedroom

4. *(pah-doosh-kah)*
Где подушка?
pillow

(pah-doosh-kah) *(nah)* *(krah-vah-tee)*
Подушка на кровати.
bed

5. *(krah-vaht)*
Где кровать?
bed

(krah-vaht) *(spahl-nyeh)*
Кровать в спальне.

6. *(krah-vaht)* *(bahl-shah-yah)* *(ee-lee)* *(mah-lyen-kah-yah)*
Кровать большая или маленькая?
bed big small

(krah-vaht) *(nyeh)* *(bahl-shah-yah)*
Кровать не большая.
not big
(mah-lyen-kah-yah)
Кроват маленькая.
small

☐ **материя** *(mah-tyair-ee-yah)* . . . . material
☐ **матч** *(mahtch)* . . . . match (game)
☐ **машина** *(mah-shee-nah)* . . . . machine (car)   **M**
☐ **медаль** *(myeh-dahl)* . . . . medal
☐ **медик** *(myeh-deek)* . . . . medic

Теперь answer **вопросы** *(vah-proh-see)* based on **картинке** *(kar-teen-kyeh)* on **странице** 54.
questions   picture

Где будильник? *(boo-deel-neek)*

Где кровать? *(krah-vaht)*

Где _____

Let's move **в** *(vuh)* **ванную** *(vahn-noo-yoo)* **и** do the same thing.
into   bathroom

умывальник *(oo-mih-vahl-neek)*
washstand

душ *(doosh)*
shower

туалет *(too-ahl-yet)*
toilet

_____

Зелёный *(zyel-yoh-nee)* **умывальник** *(oo-mih-vahl-neek)*
green

в номере. *(nohm-yair-yeh)*
hotel room

_____

Серый *(syeh-ree)* **душ** *(doosh)* **тоже** *(toh-zheh)* **в**
gray   also

номере. *(nohm-yair-yeh)*
hotel room

_____

Белый *(byel-lee)* **и зелёный** *(zyel-yoh-nee)* **туалет**
white   green

тоже в номере. *(nohm-yair-yeh)*

зеркало *(zyair-kah-lah)* _____
mirror

полотенца *(pah-lah-tyent-sah)* ПОЛОТЕНЦА
towels

красное полотенце *(krahs-nah-yeh)* _____

коричневое полотенце *(kah-reech-nyeh-vah-yeh)* _____

оранжевое полотенце *(oh-rahn-zheh-vah-yeh)* _____

Не *(nyeh)* forget to remove the next **семь** *(syem)* stickers **и** label these
not

things in your **ванной.** *(vahn-noy)*
bathroom

55

(vahn-nah-yah)
Ванная в номере.
bathroom

Study **картинку** и answer **вопросы внизу.**

Где душ?

(doosh) *(ryah-dahm)*
Душ рядом с _____.
next to   (?)

(too-ahl-yet)   *(myezh-doo)*
Где туалет? Туалет между _____ **и** _____.
between   (?)   (?)

(oo-mih-vahl-neek)   *(ryah-dahm)*
Где умывальник? Умывальник рядом с _____.
washstand   (?)

(zyair-kah-lah)   *(nahd)*
Где зеркало? Зеркало над _____.
mirror   over   (?)

(see-nee-yeh) (pah-lah-tyent-sah)
Где синие полотенца?
towels

(pah-lah-tyent-sah)(nahd)   *(nah)*
Полотенца над _____. **Полотенца на** _с т е н е_.
over   (?)   on   (?)

(vah-nah-yah)   *(vwee)*
Remember, **ванная** means a **комната** to bathe in. If **вы в ресторане и вам нужно** to use the
room   you need

lavatory, **вы** want to ask for **туалет** not for **ванная.**

Извините.

Где туалет?

Restrooms are marked **с** the letters ☐ **Д** **и** ☐ **М**.

This should be easy to remember as **М** stands for

men's, just as it does in English.

(dahm-skee)   *(moozh-skoy)*
Д = **дамский**   **и** **М** = **мужской.**
ladies'   men's

☐ **механик** *(myeh-hah-neek)* . . . . mechanic
☐ **микрофон** *(mee-krah-fohn)* . . . . microphone
☐ **миллион** *(meel-lee-ohn)* . . . . million
☐ **миниатюра** *(mee-nee-ah-tyoo-rah)* . . . . miniature   **М**
56 ☐ **миссия** *(mees-see-yah)* . . . . mission

Next stop — *(kah-bee-nyet)* **кабинет,** specifically *(stohl)* **стол** **в кабинете.** *(kah-bee-nyet-yeh)* *(chtoh)* **Что на столе?**

study   desk/table   study   what

Let's identify things that one normally finds **на столе** or strewn about **дома.**

(kah-rahn-dahsh)
карандаш
pencil

(rooch-kah)
ручка
pen

(boo-mah-gah)
бумага
paper

(pees-moh)
письмо
letter

———————————   <u>ручка</u>   ———————————   ———————————

(aht-krit-kah)
открытка
postcard

(mar-kah)
марка
stamp

(kuh-nee-gah)
книга
book

(zhoor-nahl)
журнал
magazine

———————————   ———————————   ———————————   ———————————

(gah-zyet-ah)
газета
newspaper

(ahch-kee)
очки
eyeglasses

(tee-lee-vee-zar)
телевизор
television

(kar-zee-nah)
корзина
basket

———————————   ———————————   ———————————   ———————————

М

——————————
——————————
——————————
——————————

Теперь label these things **в кабинете** *(kah-bee-nyet-yeh)* with your stickers. Do not forget to say these **слова** out loud whenever **вы** write them, **вы** see them **или вы** apply the stickers. **Теперь** identify the things **на картинке внизу** *(vnee-zoo)* by filling in each blank with the correct **русскими словами.**

1. _____

2. _____

3. _____

4. ПИСЬМО

5. _____

6. _____

7. _____

8. _____

9. _____

10. _____

Вот четыре verbs.

(prah-dah-vaht)
продавать = to sell

(pah-sih-laht)
посылать = to send

(spaht)
спать = to sleep

(zvah-neet)
звонить = to phone

_____   _____   спать   _____

Теперь fill in the blanks on the next **странице** with the correct form of these verbs. Practice saying the sentences out loud many times. Don't get discouraged! Just look at how much **вы** have already learned **и** think ahead to **икра,** *(eek-rah)* **балет и** *(bahl-yet)* adventure.
caviar

☐ **музей** *(moo-zay)*	museum	
☐ **музыка** *(moo-zih-kah)*	music	
☐ **нация** *(naht-see-yah)*	nation	**M**
☐ **не** *(nyeh)*	not, no	
☐ **—несерьёзный** *(nyeh-see-ryoz-nee)*	not serious	

(prah-dah-vaht)
продавать
to sell

Я **продаю/** _____ цветы. *(tsvet-ee)* flowers

Он **продаёт/** _____ фрукты. *(frook-tee)* fruit
Она

Мы **продаём/** _____ билеты. *(beel-yet-tee)*

Вы **продаёте/** _____ много билетов. *(mnoh-gah) (beel-yet-ohv)* many

Они **продают/** _____ открытки. *(aht-krit-kee)*

(pah-sih-laht)
посылать
to send

Я **посылаю/** _____ письмо. *(pees-moh)* letter

Он **посылает/** _____ открытку. *(aht-krit-koo)*
Она

Мы **посылаем/** _____ книгу. *(kuh-nee-goo)*

Вы **посылаете/** _____ четыре открытки. *(cheh-tir-ee) (aht-krit-kee)*

Они **посылают/** _____ три письма. *(pees-mah)*

(spaht)
спать
to sleep

Я **сплю/** _____ в спальне. *(vuh) (spahl-nyeh)* bedroom

Он **спит/** _____ на кровати. *(krah-vah-tee)*
Она

Мы **спим/** _____ в гостинице.

Вы **спите/** _____ в доме.

Они **спят/** _____ под одеялом. *(ah-dee-yah-lahm)* under blanket

(zvah-neet)
звонить
to phone

Я **звоню/** _____ в Ленинград.

Он **звонит/** _____ в США. *(shah)* U.S.A.
Она

Мы **звоним/** _____ в Канаду.

Вы **звоните/** _____ в Англию. England

Они **звонят/** _____ в Владивосток.

The word **не** *(nyeh)* not is extremely useful **по-русски**. Add **не** before a verb **и вы** negate the sentence.

я посылаю письмо. = I send a letter.

я не посылаю письмо. = I do not send a letter.

Simple, isn't it? **Теперь, вы** negate the following sentences.

Я хочу стакан воды. _____

Мы звоним в Канаду. _____

Я понимаю по-русски. _____

☐ **нейлон** *(nay-lohn)* . . . . nylon		_____
☐ **нет!** *(nyet)* . . . . no!	**Н**	_____
☐ **никель** *(neek-yehl)* . . . . nickel		_____
☐ **норма** *(nor-mah)* . . . . norm, standard		_____
☐ **нос** *(nohs)* . . . . nose		_____

Step 15

^(poach-tah)
Почта
mail

Теперь вы ^(vwee) know **как** ^(kahk) to count, **как** to ask **вопросы,** ^(vah-proh-see) **как** to use verbs **с** ^(suh) the "plug-in"

formula, **как** to make statements, **и как** to describe something, be it the location of

гостиница или цвет ^(tsvet) **дома.** Let's now take the basics that **вы** have learned **и** expand them
color of house

in special areas that will be most helpful in your travels. What does everyone do on a

holiday? Send **открытки,** ^(aht-krit-kee) of course! Let's learn exactly **как русское почтовое** ^(poach-toh-vah-yeh)
post

отделение, ^(aht-dyel-yen-ee-yeh) commonly called „**почта,**" ^(poach-tah) works.
office

Почта...
mail

в Америку
to

в Испанию ^(ee-spahn-ee-yoo)

в Англию ^(ahn-glee-yoo)

в Италию ^(ee-tah-lee-yoo)

Почта is where **вы** need to go **в СССР** to buy **марки** ^(mar-kee) **и конверты,** ^(kahn-vyair-tee) mail a package, send
envelopes

a telegram or use **телефон. Вот** ^(voht) some necessary **слова для** ^(dil-yah) **почты.** ^(poach-tee) Be sure to practice
here are for post office

them out loud **и тогда** ^(tahg-dah) write **слова под** ^(pohd) **картинкой.** ^(kar-teen-koy)
under

конверт ^(kahn-vyairt)
envelope

открытка ^(aht-krit-kah)
postcard

марка ^(mar-kah)
stamp

телеграмма ^(teh-leh-grahm-mah)

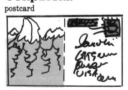

_____   открытка   _____   _____

O

_____
_____
_____
_____
_____

(pah-sil-kah)
посылка
package

(putch-toh-vee) (yah'sh-chik)
почтовый ящик
mailbox

(ah-vee-ah-poach-toy)
авиапочтой
by airmail

АВИАПОЧТОЙ

(ahk-noh)
окно
window

_____   _____   _____   _____

(teh-leh-fohn-ahv-toh-maht)
телефон-автомат
public telephone

(teh-leh-fohn)
телефон
telephone

(poach-tah)
почта
post office

ПОЧТА

_____   телефон   _____

Почта в СССР has everything. **Вы** send **посылки,** *(pah-sil-kee)* **письма** *(pees-mah)* **и открытки** *(aht-krit-kee)* **с почты.** *(poach-tee)*
packages   letters   postcards   from

Вы buy **марки на** *(nah)* **почте. Вы** can send **телеграмму с почты.** *(teh-leh-grahm-moo)* **Почта** is generally **открыта** *(aht-krit-ah)*
at   telegram   open

с 9-ти *(suh) (tee)* **часов** *(chah-sohv)* **утра** *(oo-trah)* **до** *(doh)* **20-ти** *(tee)* **часов вечера.** *(vyeh-cheh-rah)* **По** *(poh)* **субботам** *(soo-boh-tahm)* **и воскресеньям,** *(voh-skree-syen-yahm)*
from   o'clock   morning   until   evening   on   Saturdays   Sundays

почта закрыта. *(zah-krit-ah)* If **вам** *(vahm)* **нужно** *(noozh-nah)* to send **телеграмму в США** *(shah)* **или Канаду,** *(kah-nah-doo)* this can be done
closed   you need   telegram   U.S.A.

на почте. *(poach-too)* Let's go to **почту.** Okay. First step—enter **почту.**
at

The following is **хороший** *(hah-roh-shee)* sample **диалога.** *(dee-ah-loh-gah)* Familiarize yourself **с** these **словами.** *(sloh-vah-mee)* Don't
good   dialogue

wait until your holiday.

Извините. Где я могу купить конверты?

Окно семь.

ОКНО 7

☐ **опера** *(oh-pyeh-rah)*.....................	opera
☐ **органист** *(ar-gah-neest)*.................	organist
☐ **оркестр** *(ar-kyes-ter)*..................	orchestra
☐ **офицер** *(ah-feet-syair)*................	officer
☐ **официальный** *(ah-feet-see-ahl-nih)*......	official

о

_____
_____
_____
_____
_____

Я хочу купить конверты для двух (2) писем в США и двух (2) открыток в Англию.

Авиапочтой?

Конверты тридцать пять копеек (35 коп.) и открытки десять копеек (10 коп.)

Сколько это стоит?

Да, авиапочтой, пожалуйста. Я хочу купить марки для двух писем в Одессу. Сколько это стоит?

Шесть копеек (6 коп.).

Да, хорошо.

Вот марки. Это один рубль и две копейки.

Спасибо.

Next step—**вы** ask **вопросы** like those **внизу,** depending on what **вы хотите.**
(hah-teet-yeh)
would like

Где я могу   купить марки?
(mah-goo) (koo-peet) (mar-kee)
I   can   buy

Где я могу   послать телеграмму?
(mah-goo)(pah-slaht)   (teh-leh-grahm-moo)
send

Где я могу купить открытку?
(aht-krit-koo)

Где я могу послать посылку?
(pah-sil-koo)
package

Где телефон?

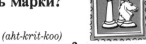

Где я могу звонить в США?
(zvah-neet)   (shah)
phone   U.S.A.

Где почтовый   ящик?
(putch-toh-vee)   (yahsh-chik)
mailbox

Сколько это стоит?
(stoy-eet)
costs

Где телефон-автомат?
public telephone

Где я могу звонить в Ялту?
(zvah-neet)   (yahl-too)
Yalta

(pohv-tah-ryah-ee-tee)
Повторяйте the above sentences many times.
repeat

Теперь, quiz yourself. See if **вы** can translate the following thoughts **на русский.**

Ответы are at the bottom of the next **страницы.**

1.   Where is a public telephone? _____

2.   Where can I phone? _____

3.   Where can I phone to the U.S.A.? _____

4.   Where can I phone to Leningrad? _____

5.   Where is the post office? _____

62

6. Where can I buy stamps? _____

7. Airmail envelopes? _____

8. Where can I send a package? _____

9. Where can I send a telegram? _____

10. Where is window eight? _____

(voht)
Вот are more verbs.

(die-tee) **дайте** = give (me)   *(pee-saht)* **писать** = to write   *(pah-kah-zih-vaht)* **показывать** = to show   *(plah-teet) (zah)* **платить за** = to pay for

_____

(die-tee)
дайте
give (me)

Дайте мне	*(pah-zhahl-yes-tah)* пожалуйста, *(shyoht)* счёт.
	bill
_____	*(ah-dres)* пожалуйста, адрес.
	address
_____	*(sdah-choo)* пожалуйста, сдачу.
	change
Дайте мне	пожалуйста, меню.
_____	пожалуйста, билет.

(pee-saht)
писать
to write

Я	пишу/	письмо.
Он Она	пишет/	*(mnoh-gah)* много.
		a lot
Мы	пишем/	телеграмму.
Вы	пишете/	*(ah-dres)* адрес.
Они	пишут/	открытку.

(pah-kah-zih-vaht)
показывать
to show

Я	показываю/	*(vahm)* вам книгу.
		to you
Он Она	показывает/	*(men-yeh)* мне Кремль.
		to me
Мы	показываем/	*(vahm) (moo-zay)* вам музей.
		to you
Вы	показываете/	*(men-yeh)* мне письмо.
		to me letter
Они	показывают/	мне почту.

(plah-teet) (zah)
платить за
to pay   for

Я	плачу за/	*(res-tah-rahn-nee) (shyoht)* ресторанный счёт.
		restaurant bill
Он Она	платит за/	*(gah-stee-neech-nee)* гостиничный счёт.
Мы	платим за/	*(beel-yet-tee) (tee-ah-ter)* билеты в театр.
		tickets theater
Вы	платите за/	*(bahl-yet)* билеты на балет.
Они	платят за/	*(kahn-tsairt)* билеты на концерт.
		concert

63

Step 16

(kahk) *(plah-teet)*
Как Платить
how   to pay

Да, there are also *(shyoh-tah)* **счёта** to pay **в СССР.** **Вы** have just finished your delicious dinner и

(hah-teet-yeh) *(shyoht)*   *(moh-zhet-yeh)* *(plah-teet)*   *(ah-feet-see-ahn-tah)*
вы хотите **счёт.** **Как вы можете платить?** **Вы** call for **официанта: „Официант!"**
would like   bill   bills   can   pay   waiter

> Извините. Дайте, пожалуйста, счёт.

> Да, одну минуту, пожалуйста.

(ah-feet-see-ahnt)
Официант will normally reel off what **вы** have
waiter

eaten, while writing rapidly. **Он** will then place

(shyoht) *(stohl)*
счёт на стол that looks something like the one
bill

на картинке, while saying something like

(roo-blay)
> „**Вот счёт. Восемь рублей, пожалуйста.**"
> here is

(ah-feet-see-ahn-too)
Вы will pay **официанту** или perhaps **вы** will pay **кассиру.**
cashier   *(kahs-see-roo)*

(mwee)   *(nyet)*
Being a seasoned traveler, **вы** know that tipping as **мы** know it **в США и Канаде нет** a
is not

(shyoht-yeh)
custom **в СССР.** Generally the service is included **в счёте.**

> Хороший обед, спасибо.

> Пожалуйста, до свидания.

If **вы** are planning to dine out **в СССР, вы**

should definitely make reservations. It can be

(res-tah-rahn)
very difficult to get into a popular **ресторан.**

Nevertheless, the experience is well worth the

trouble **вы** will go to to obtain a reservation.

И remember, **вы** know enough **русский** to make

a reservation.

☐ **парк** *(park)*	park		_____
☐ **парламент** *(par-lah-myent)*	parliament		_____
☐ **партия** *(par-tee-yah)*	party	**П**	_____
☐ **паспорт** *(pahs-port)*	passport		_____
☐ **пассажир** *(pahs-sah-zheer)*	passenger		_____

Remember these key **слова** when dining out **в СССР**.

(myen-yoo)
МЕНЮ
menu

(shyoht)
СЧЁТ
bill

(ah-feet-see-ahnt)
официант
waiter

(kvee-tahn-tsee-yah)
КВИТАНЦИЯ
receipt

(sdah-chah)
сдача
change

(ah-feet-see-ahnt-kah)
официантка
waitress

Politeness is **очень важна в СССР**. **Вы** will feel more **как русский** if **вы** practice **и**
(oh-cheen) (vazh-nah)   like   (a) Russian

use these expressions.

(eez-vee-nee-tee)
ИЗВИНИТЕ
excuse me

(pah-zhahl-yes-tah)
пожалуйста
please

(spah-see-bah)
спасибо
thank you

(pah-zhahl-yes-tah)
пожалуйста
you're welcome

Вот a sample conversation involving paying **счёт когда** leaving **гостиницу**.
(shyoht)

(zee-nah)
Зина: **Извините. Я хочу оплатить счёт.**
(oh-plah-teet)
    to pay

(ahd-mee-nee-strah-tor)
Администратор: **Номер, пожалуйста?**
(nohm-yair) (pah-zhahl-yes-tah)
number

Зина: **Номер триста десять.**
(nohm-yair)(tree-stah) (dyes-yet)
number

Администратор: **Спасибо. Одну минуту, пожалуйста.**
(ahd-noo)

Администратор: **Вот счёт. Сорок пять рублей, пожалуйста.**
(so-rahk)   *(roo-blay)*

Зина: **Спасибо. (И Зина** hands him **пятьдесят рублей. Администратор**

returns shortly **и говорит...)**
(gah-vah-reet)

Администратор: **Вот ваша квитанция и ваша сдача. Спасибо и до свидания.**
(vah-shah)(kvee-tahn-tsee-yah)   *(vah-shah)(sdah-chah)*   *(doh) (svee-dahn-ee-yah)*
your   receipt   your   change   goodbye

Simple, right? If **вы** have any problems **с числами,** just ask someone to write out
(chee-slah-mee)
numbers

(chee-slah)
числа, so that **вы** can be sure you understand everything correctly.

Пожалуйста напишите числа. Спасибо.
(nah-pee-sheet-yeh)
write out

Let's take a break from **денег и,** starting on the next **странице,** learn some **новые** fun
(dyen-yeg)   *(noh-vih-yeh)*

слова.

- ☐ **программа** *(proh-grah-mah)* .... program
- ☐ **позиция** *(pah-zeet-see-yah)* .... position
- ☐ **полиция** *(pah-leet-see-yah)* .... police   **П**
- ☐ **порт** *(port)* .... port
- ☐ **портрет** *(port-ryet)* .... portrait

(zdah-rohv)
Он здоров.
healthy

(bohl-yen)
Он болен.
sick

(hah-rah-shoh)
Это хорошо.
good

(nyeh)
Это не хорошо.
not good

(ploh-hah)
Это плохо.
bad

(vah-dah) (gar-yah-chah-yah)
Вода горячая -
water hot

(grah-doo-sohv)
тридцать пять градусов.
degrees

35°

(hah-lohd-nah-yah)
Вода холодная -
cold

пять градусов.

5°

ГРОМКО

ТИХО

(gah-vah-ree-tee)(grohm-kah)
Вы говорите громко.
speak   loudly

(gah-vah-reet) (tee-hah)
Он говорит тихо.
speaks   softly

(lee-nee-yah)(kah-roht-kah-yah)
Красная линия короткая.
line   short

(dleen-nah-yah)
Синяя линия длинная.
long

(zhen-shchee-nah) (vwee-soh-kah-yah)
Женщина высокая.
woman   tall

(ryeb-yoh-nahk) (mah-lyen-kee)
Ребёнок маленький.
child   small/short

(nahd)
над

(lyev-ah)
лево

(prah-vah)
право

(pohd)
под

Красная книга толстая.
(tohl-stah-yah)
thick

Зелёная книга тонкая.
(tohn-kah-yah)
green   thin

(kee-loh-myeh-trohv) (chahs)
20 километров в час

200 километров в час

(myed-lyen-nah)
медленно
slow

(bis-trah)
быстро
fast

☐ **прогресс** *(prohg-ryes)* .... progress
☐ **продукт** *(proh-dookt)* .... product
☐ **проект** *(proh-yekt)* .... project   **П**
☐ **профессия** *(prah-fyes-see-yah)* .... profession
☐ **профессор** *(prah-fyes-sar)* .... professor

(goh-rih) *(vwee-soh-kee-yeh)* *(tees-yah-chee)*
Горы высокие — две тысячи метров.
mountains / high / two thousand / meters

(neez-kee-yeh) *(tohl-kah)* *(voh-syem-soht)*
Горы низкие — только восемьсот метров.
low / only

(dyed) *(stah-ree)* *(syem-dyes-yet)* *(lyet)*
Дед старый. Ему семьдесят лет.
old / to him / seventy / years

(sin) *(mah-lah-doy)*
Сын молодой. Ему только десять лет.
son / young / only

(doh-rah-gah-yah)(stoy-eet) *(roo-blay)*
Комната в гостинице дорогая. Стоит 30 рублей.
expensive

(pahn-see-oh-naht) *(dyeh-shyoh-vwee)*
Пансионат дешёвый. Стоит 15 рублей.
boarding house/inn / inexpensive

(oo) *(men-yah)* *(boh-gaht)* *(mnoh-gah)* *(dyen-yeg)*
У меня есть сто рубдей. Я богат. У меня есть много денег.
rich / a lot / money

(nyeh-voh) *(roob-lyah)* *(byed-yen)* *(mah-lah)*
У него есть три рубля. Он беден. У него есть мало денег.
he / has / poor / little

3 руб.
100 р.

Вот новые verbs.

(znaht)
знать = to know
(e.g., a fact, an address)

(mohch)
мочь = to be able to/can

(chee-taht)
читать = to read

(poot-yeh-shest-vah-vaht)
путешествовать = to travel

_____   _____   читать   _____

Notice that some verbs change slightly by adding a „за-" или „по-." Don't panic.

This does not change the basic meaning of the word. **Вот два** examples. Learn to listen

for the core of the verb. For example, note the word „платить" within „заплатить за."

(plah-teet) **платить**—*(oh-plah-teet)* **оплатить**—*(zah-plah-teet)* **заплатить** *(zah)* **за**	*(koo-peet)* **купить** — *(pah-koo-paht)* **покупать**
to pay / to pay / to pay / for	to buy / to buy
(plah-choo) **Я плачу десять рублей.**	*(mar-kee)* **Я хочу купить марки.**
(shyoht) **Я хочу оплатить счёт.**	*(kuh-nee-goo)* **Я хочу купить книгу.**
(zah-plah-choo) **Я заплачу за обед.** meal	*(pah-koo-pah-yoo)(zhoor-nahl)* **Я покупаю журнал.**

☐ **процент** *(praht-syent)* . . . . percent
☐ **радио** *(rah-dee-oh)* . . . . radio
☐ **ракета** *(rah-kyet-ah)* . . . . rocket
☐ **ранг** *(rahng)* . . . . rank
☐ **рапорт** *(rah-port)* . . . . report

р

_____
_____
_____
_____
_____

Study the patterns **внизу** closely, as **вы** will use these verbs a lot.

(znaht)
знать
to know

Я __знаю/_____ **всё.**
(vsyoh) everything

Он __знает/_____ **адрес.**
Она *(ah-dres)* address

Мы __знаем/__ **как** **говорить по-русски.**
(gah-vah-reet) how to speak

Вы __знаете/__ **название** **гостиницы.**
(nahz-vah-nee-yeh) name

Они __знают/__ **название ресторана.**
(res-tah-rah-nah)

(mohch)
мочь
to be able to/can

Я __могу/_____ **говорить по-русски.**
(gah-vah-reet) speak

Он __может/__ **понимать по-английски.**
Она *(poh-nee-maht)* understand

Мы __можем/_____ **понимать по-русски.**

Вы __можете/_____ **говорить по-английски.**

Они __могут/__ **говорить по-русски** **тоже.**
(toh-zheh) also

(chee-taht)
читать
to read

Я __читаю/_____ **книгу.**

Он __читает/_____ **журнал.**
Она magazine

Мы __читаем/_____ **меню.**

Вы __читаете/_____ **много.**
a lot

Они __читают/_____ **газету.**
newspaper

(poot-yeh-shest-vah-vaht)
путешествовать
to travel

Я __путешествую/_____ **в** **январе.**
(vuh) (yahn-var-yeh) January

Он __путешествует/_____ **зимой.**
Она *(zee-moy)* in winter

Мы __путешествуем/_____ **в июле.**
(ee-yool-yeh) July

Вы __путешествуете/_____ **летом.**
(lyet-ahm) in summer

Они __путешествуют/_____ **весной.**
(vees-noy) in spring

(mohzh-yet-yeh)
Вы можете translate the sentences **внизу на русский?** **Ответы внизу.**
can   into

1. I can speak Russian. _____

2. They can pay the bill._____

3. He needs to pay the bill._____

4. We know the address.__Мы   знаем   адрес.__

5. She knows a lot. _____

6. We can read Russian. _____

Теперь, draw **линию** *(lee-nee-yoo)* **между** *(myezh-doo)* the opposites **внизу.** **Не** forget to say them out loud. Use
lines between

эти слова *(et-tee)* every day to describe **вещи в доме,** *(vesh-chee)* **в школе,** *(shkohl-yeh)* at work, etc.
home school

(vwee-soh-kah-yah)
высокая

(lyev-ah)
лево

(mah-lah-doy)
молодой

(byed-yen)
беден

(zdah-rohv)
здоров

(dleen-nah-yah)
длинная

(mnoh-gah)
много

(hah-rah-shoh)
хорошо

(tohl-stah-yah)
толстая

(vwee-soh-kee-yeh)
высокие

(gah-yah-chah-yah)
горячая

(pohd)
под

(myed-lyen-nah)
медленно

(dah-rah-gah-yah)
дорогая

(tee-hah)
тихо

(nahd)
над

(neez-kee-yeh)
низкие

(kah-roht-kah-yah)
короткая

(grohm-kah)
громко

(tohn-kah-yah)
тонкая

(dyeh-shoh-vwee)
дешёвый

(mah-lah)
мало

(bohl-yen)
болен

(stah-ree)
старый

(bis-trah)
быстро

(prah-vah)
право

(hah-lohd-nah-yah)
холодная

(bah-gaht)
богат

(ploh-hah)
плохо

(mah-lyen-kee)
маленький

Теперь вы знаете что „**большой**" means large **по-русски.** Haven't **вы** heard of the world-
that

famous „**Большой Театр**"? In addition to being one of the world's foremost ballet

companies, it is also **старейший** *(star-yeh-shee)* **московский театр.** It is a must to see **когда вы** are **в Москве.**
oldest

If **вы** travel **в Ленинград, тогда** visit **театр оперы** *(oh-pyair-ee)* **и балета** called **С.М. Кирова.** *(kee-rah-vah)*
then (of) opera Kirov

Step 17

(poot-yeh-shest-vah-vaht)
Путешествовать
to travel

(vchee-rah) *(lee-neen-grahd-yeh)*
Вчера в Ленинграде!
yesterday

(see-vohd-nyah) *(nohv-gah-rahd-yeh)*
Сегодня в Новгороде!
today

(zahv-trah) *(smahl-yensk-yeh)*
Завтра в Смоленске!

If you know a few key **слова,** traveling can be easy, clean **и очень** efficient **в СССР.**
(oh-cheen) very

(pyaht-nod-tset)
В Советском Союзе пятнадцать republics. **СССР** is 6,000 miles wide which is equivalent

(myezh-doo)
to the distance **между** California **и** France, **и** it has **одиннадцать** time zones. This can
between
(ah-deen-nud-tset)

make traveling **в СССР** a major undertaking.

(yed-yet)
Иван едет на машине.
Ivan goes

(lee-teet) *(sah-mahl-yoht-yeh)*
Борис летит на самолёте.
flies airplane

(ee-ree-nah) *(moh-tah-tsee-kul-yeh)*
Ирина едет на мотоцикле.
motorcycle

(poh-yezd-yeh)
Нина едет на поезде.
train

(myeh-troh)
Зина едет на метро.
subway

(veek-tor)
Виктор едет на автобусе.

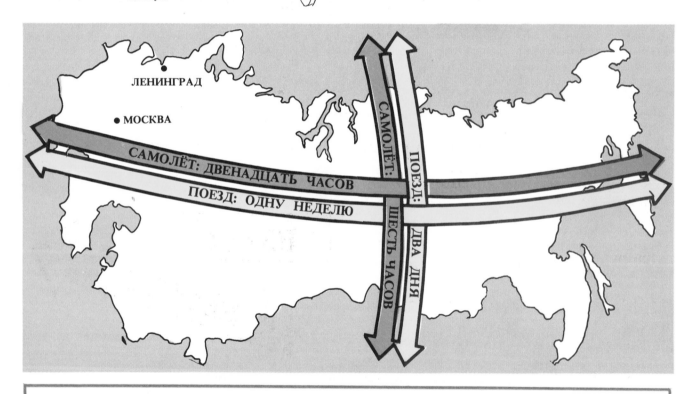

ЛЕНИНГРАД

● МОСКВА

САМОЛЁТ: ДВЕНАДЦАТЬ ЧАСОВ

ПОЕЗД: ОДНУ НЕДЕЛЮ

САМОЛЁТ: ШЕСТЬ ЧАСОВ

ПОЕЗД: ДВА ДНЯ

(vee-deet-yeh) *(nah-vyair-hoo)*
Вы видите карту наверху? Это СССР. Ехать с севера на юг, занимает шесть
do you see map
(yek-haht) *(syev-yair-ah)* *(yoog)* *(zah-nee-mah-yet)*
to go from north to south it takes

(den-yah)
часов на самолёте, и два дня на поезде. Это не плохо.
days bad

☐ **салат** *(sah-laht)*........................ salad
☐ **самовар** *(sah-mah-var)*............... samovar
☐ **сезон** *(syeh-zone)*..................... season
☐ **секунда** *(syek-oon-dah)*.............. second
☐ **семинар** *(syem-ee-nar)*.............. seminar

с

70

Русские любят путешествовать, *(loob-yaht)* *(poot-yeh-shest-vah-vaht)* so **это не** *(nyeh)* surprise to find **много слов** revolving around
love

the concept of travel which is exactly what **вы хотите** *(hah-teet-yeh)* to do. Practice saying the
want

following **слова** many times. **Вы** will see them **часто.** *(chah-stah)*
often

(pah-yezd-kah)
поездка
journey, trip

(poot-yeh-shest-vah-vaht)
путешествовать
to travel

(poot-yeh-shest-vyen-neek)
путешественник
traveler

(lee-tyet)
лететь на самолёте
to fly

ехать на машине
to go

ехать на поезде

ехать на автобусе
bus

ехать на мотоцикле

(myeh-troh)
ехать на метро
subway

(eed-tee)
идти
to walk

(byoo-roh) *(poot-yeh-shest-vee-ee)*
бюро путешествий
travel agency

(schahst-lee-vah-vah) *(poo-tee)*
Счастливого пути!
have a good trip

Внизу *(vnee-zoo)* some basic signs which **вам нужно знать.** *(vahm)* *(noozh-nah)* *(znaht)* Most of these **слов** come from the
to know

verbs, **входить** *(vhah-deet)* = to enter **и выходить** *(vwee-hah-deet)* = to go out/to exit.

(vhohd)
ВХОД _____
entrance

(glahv-nee)
главный вход _____
main   entrance

(vhoh-dah)
входа нет ВХОДа НеТ_____
do not enter

(vwee-hahd)
ВЫХОД _____
exit

(zah-pahs-noy)
запасной выход _____
emergency   exit

(oht) *(syeb-yah)*
от себя_____
push (doors)

(kuh) *(syeb-yeh)*
к себе_____
pull (doors)

ВХОД

ВЫХОД

ОТ СЕБЯ

К СЕБЕ

☐ **сигара** *(see-gah-rah)*. . . . . cigar _____
☐ **сигарета** *(see-gah-ryet-ah)*. . . . . cigarette _____
☐ **симфония** *(seem-foh-nee-yah)*. . . . . symphony **с** _____
☐ **советский** *(sah-vyet-skee)*. . . . . Soviet _____
☐ **стадион** *(stah-dee-ohn)*. . . . . stadium _____

(yek-haht) „**Ехать**" is **очень** *(vazh-nee)* **важный** verb *(dil-yah)* **для** *(too-rees-tah)* **туриста.** If **вы** choose **ехать на машине, вот** a few key

слов.

(shohs-syeh)
шоссе ___шоссе, шоссе___
main road

(mah-shee-nah)(nah-prah-kaht)
машина напрокат _____
rental car

(dah-roh-gah)
дорога в Ленинград _____
road

(byoo-roh) *(prah-kah-tah)*
бюро проката _____
car rental agency

(oo-leet-sah)
улица _____
street

(ahv-tah-stahnt-see-yah)
автостанция _____
service station

Вот четыре очень important opposites.

Ленинград - Москва		
(aht-hah-deet) **Отходит** departs	**Поезд No.**	*(pree-dyoht)* **Придёт** arrives
0:41	50	12:41
7:40	19	19:40
12:15	10	0:15
14:32	4	2:32
21:40	22	9:40

(pree-yezd)
приезд _____
arrival

(aht-prahv-lyen-ee-yeh)
отправление _____
departure

(ee-nah-strahn-nee)
иностранный _____
foreign

(myest-nee)
местный ___местный___
domestic/internal

Let's learn the basic travel verbs. Follow the same pattern **вы** have in previous steps.

(lee-tyet)
лететь = to fly

___лететь___

(prah-veet)
править = to drive

_____

(zah-kah-zih-vaht)
заказывать = to reserve/
order

_____

(pree-yez-zhaht)
приезжать = to arrive

_____

(oo-yez-zhaht)
уезжать = to leave

_____

(dyeh-laht)
делать = to make

_____

(ah-pahz-dih-vaht)
опаздывать = to be late

_____

(dyeh-laht) *(pyair-yeh-sahd-koo)*
делать пересадку = to
make a transfer

_____

(oo-klah-dih-vaht)
укладывать = to pack

_____

(pree-hah-deet)
приходить = to arrive
(trains, buses, ships)

_____

(aht-hah-deet)
отходить = to depart
(trains, buses, ships)

_____

☐ **старт** *(start)*................... start
☐ **студент** *(stoo-dyent)*........... student
☐ **суп** *(soup)*.................. soup
☐ **табак** *(tah-bahk)*............. tobacco
☐ **такси** *(tahk-see)*............. taxi

Т _____
_____
_____
_____
_____

72

С these verbs, **вы** are ready for any trip anywhere. **Вы** should have no problem **с** these verbs, just remember the basic "plug-in" formula **вы** have already learned. Use that knowledge to translate the following thoughts **на русский**. **Ответы внизу**.
into

1. I fly to the Soviet Union. _____

2. I make a transfer in Moscow. _____

3. He arrives in Yalta. _____

4. We leave tomorrow. _____

5. We reserve tickets to Kiev. _____

6. They drive to Novgorod. _____

7. Where is the train to Odessa? _____

8. How can I fly to the Soviet Union? On British Airways or Aeroflot? _____

_____

(noh-vih-yeh) *(dil-yah)* *(pah-yezd-kee)*
Вот some **новые слова для поездки**. As always, write out **слова и** practice the sample

sentences out loud.

(plaht-for-mah)
платформа
platform

(vahk-zahl)
вокзал
train station

(air-oh-drohm)
аэродром
airport

_____

ВОКЗАЛ

_____

**Извините. Где
платформа номер два?**

Извините. Где вокзал?

Извините. Где аэродром?

(bahnk)
банк
bank

_____

Извините. Где банк?

(byoo-roh) (nah-hoh-dahk)
бюро находок
office for   lost-and-found

_____

Извините. Где бюро находок?

(rah-spee-sah-nee-yeh)
расписание   поездов
timetable

Ленинград - Москва		
(aht-hah-deet) **Отходит** departs	**Поезд No.**	*(pree-dyoht)* **Придёт** arrives
0:41	50	12:41
7:40	19	19:40
12:15	10	0:15
14:32	4	2:32
21:40	22	9:40

_____

Извините. Где расписание поездов?

(zahn-yah-tah)
занято _____

occupied
(svah-bohd-nah)
свободно _____

free
(vah-gohn)
вагон _____

compartment/wagon
(myes-tah)
место *место, место, место*

seat/place
(et-tah)
Это место занято? _____

Это место свободно? _____

(et-tut) (vah-gohn) (zahn-yaht)
Этот вагон занят? _____

this
(svah-bohd-yen)
Этот вагон свободен? _____

Practice writing out the following **вопросы.** It will help you **позже.**
(pohzh-yeh)
later

Извините. Где туалет? _____

(vah-gohn-res-tah-rahn)
Извините. Где вагон-ресторан? _____
dining compartment

(zahl) *(ah-zhee-dahn-ee-yah)*
Где зал ожидания? *Где зал ожидания?*
waiting room

Где окно номер восемь? _____
window
(mohzh-nah) (koo-reet)
Можно курить? _____
is it possible   to smoke

НЕ КУРИТЬ! _____
no   smoking

☐ **театр** *(teh-ah-ter)*	theater	_____
☐ **телевизор** *(teh-leh-vee-zor)*	television	_____
☐ **телеграмма** *(teh-leh-grahm-mah)*	telegram	**Т**
☐ **телескоп** *(tel-leh-skope)*	telescope	_____
☐ **телефон** *(teh-leh-fohn)*	telephone	_____

74

Increase your travel **слова** by writing out **слова внизу и** practicing the sample sentences out loud. Practice asking „**где**" questions.

(vuh)
в _____

to

Где поезд в Москву?

(poot)
путь _____

line/route

Где путь номер семь?

(kah-myair-ah)(hrahn-yen-ee-yah)
камера   хранения _____

left-luggage   office

Где...?

(nah-seelsh-cheek)
носильщик _____

porter

Где носильщик?

(vreh-mee-nee)
времени _____

time

У меня мало времени.

(sprah-vahch-nah-yeh)(byoo-roh)
справочное   бюро_____

information bureau

Где...?

(tah-mohzh-nyah)
таможня _таможня_

customs

Где таможня?

(kahs-sah)
касса _____

tickets/cashier

Где касса?

Practice these **слова** every day. **Вы** will be surprised **как** *(chahs-tah)* **часто вы** will use them.

often

(mohzh-yet-yeh) (prah-chee-taht)
Вы можете   прочитать the following paragraph?

can   read

Вы теперь в самолёте *(sah-mahl-yoht-yeh)* **и вы** *(lee-teet-yeh)* **летите в СССР. У** *(oo)* **вас** *(vahs)* **есть деньги** *(dyen-gee)* (you do, don't you?),

fly   you   have

билеты, паспорт, виза и чемодан. *(pahs-port)* *(vee-zah)* *(cheh-mah-dahn)* **Теперь вы турист. Вы приедете** *(too-reest)* **завтра в пять часов** *(pree-yed-yet-yeh)*

passport   visa   suitcases   arrive

в СССР. Счастливого   пути! *(schahst-lee-vah-vah) (poo-tee)*

В СССР, there are **два** main types of **поезда.** **Пригородные   поезда,** *(pree-gah-rahd-nee-yeh)* called „**электрички,**" *(el-ek-treech-kee)*

suburban

provide the main transportation from **пригородов** *(pree-gah-rah-dahv)* to **центра** *(tsen-trah)* **города.** *(gah-rah-dah)* **Междугородные** *(myezh-doo-gah-rahd-nee-yeh)*

suburbs   center   (of) city   inter-city/long distance

поезда travel longer distances, **между** *(myezh-doo)* **городами.** *(gah-rah-dah-mee)* If **вы путешествуете** *(poot-yeh-shest-voo-yet-yeh)* **из Москвы в**

between   cities   travel   from

Ленинград, или из Москвы в Владивосток, вы may want to catch **скорый поезд** *(skor-ee)* that

express

travels faster **и** makes no intermediate stops.

Some **поезда** have **вагоны-рестораны и** some **поезда** have **спальные вагоны.** *(spahl-nee-yeh)* All this will be

sleeping   wagons

indicated on your **расписание,** *(rah-spee-sah-nee-yeh)* but remember **вы знаете как** *(znah-yet-yeh)* to ask things like this.

timetable   know

Practice your possible **вопросы** combinations by writing out the following samples.

(spahl-nee)
Где спальный вагон? _____

sleeping   compartment/wagon

(boof-yet)
Где   буфет? _____

snack car

☐ **теннис** *(tyen-nees)*..................... tennis			_____
☐ **три** *(tree)*.............................. three			_____
☐ **томат** *(tah-maht)*...................... tomato	**Т**		_____
☐ **тост** *(toast)*............................ toast			_____
☐ **турист** *(toor-eest)*...................... tourist			_____

What about inquiring about the price of **билетов?** *(beel-yet-tohv)* tickets **Вы можете** *(mohzh-yet-yeh)* can ask **вопросы.**

Сколько стоит билет в Ленинград? *(beel-yet)* _____

В одном направлении *(ahd-nohm)(nah-prahv-lyen-ee-ee)* one-way _____ **туда и обратно** *(too-dah)(ahb-raht-nah)* there and back _____

Сколько стоит билет в Одессу? *(oh-des-soo)* _____

Сколько стоит билет в Москву? *(mahsk-voo)* _____

Туда и обратно? *(ahb-raht-nah)* ~~Туда и обратно?~~

What about times of **отправления и прибытия?** *(aht-prahv-lyen-ee-yah)* departures *(pree-beet-ee-yah)* arrivals **Вы тоже можете** *(toh-zheh)* ask these **вопросы.**

Когда я могу ехать на поезде в Ташкент? *(kahg-dah)* when *(mah-goo)* can *(yek-haht)* go *(tahsh-kyent)* _____

Когда я могу лететь на самолёте в Москву? *(lee-tyet)* *(sah-mahl-yoht-yeh)* _____

Когда я могу лететь на самолёте во Владывосток? *(voh)(vlah-dee-vah-stohk)* _____

Когда придёт поезд из Риги? *(pree-dyoht)* arrives *(ree-gee)* from Riga _____

Когда придёт поезд из Баку? *(bah-koo)* Baku _____

Вы have just arrived **в СССР. Вы теперь на вокзале.** *(vahk-zahl-yeh)* at **Вы хотите ехать в Ленинград?** *(hah-teet-yeh)* want to go

В Киев? *(kee-yev)* Kiev **В Москву?** Well, tell that to the person at **окна** selling **билеты.** window

Я хочу поехать в Новгород. *(hah-choo)(pah-yek-haht)* *(nohv-gah-rahd)* _____

Я хочу поехать в Ялту. *(yahl-too)* Yalta ~~Я хочу поехать в Ялту.~~

Я хочу поехать в Одессу. *(oh-des-soo)* Odessa _____

Когда я могу ехать на поезда в Одессу? *(mah-goo)* _____

Сколько стоит билет в Одессу? _____

Я хочу купить билет в Одессу. _____

Туда и обратно? *(ahb-raht-nah)* _____

Мне нужно сделать пересадку? *(men-yeh)(noozh-nah)* I need *(sdyeh-laht)* to make *(pyair-yeh-sahd-koo)* a transfer _____ **Спасибо.** *(spah-see-bah)* _____

С this practice, **вы** are off **и** running. These travel **слова** will make your holiday twice as

enjoyable **и** at least three times as easy. Review these **новые слова** by doing the crossword

76 puzzle **на странице** *(nah)* 77. Practice drilling yourself on this Step by selecting other locations и asking your own **вопросы** about **поездах,** *(poh-yez-dahk)* **автобусах** *(ahv-toh-boo-sahk)* или **самолётах** *(sah-mahl-yoh-tahk)* that go

there. Select **новые слова из** *(eez)* **словаря** *(slah-var-yah)* и practice asking questions that begin **с**
from   dictionary

| ГДЕ | КОГДА | СКОЛЬКО | КАК ЧАСТО | или making statements like |

ACROSS

1. to arrive
2. station
3. platform
4. excuse me
5. main road
6. compartment/wagon
7. to eat
8. one
9. thank-you
10. arrival
11. eastern
12. cat
13. customs
14. under
15. fast
16. domestic/internal
17. to order/reserve
18. street
19. bank
20. motorcycle

DOWN

3. traveler
8. departure
14. to drink
16. menu
21. restaurant
22. to go/to ride
23. or
24. tomorrow
25. over
26. schedule
27. airport
28. left
29. mail/post office
30. to open
31. porter
32. give!
33. taxi
34. toilet

Я хочу поехать в Смоленск.
Я хочу купить билет.

(crossword grid with entries including ПЛАТФОРМА, УЛИЦА)

Step 18

(myen-yoo)
Меню
menu

(oo) (vahs) *(gah-lohd-nee)* *(hah-teet-yeh) (yest)* *(hah-rah-shee)*
Вы теперь в СССР и у вас есть номер. Вы голодны. Вы хотите есть. Где хороший
you have / hungry / to eat / good

(res-tah-rahn)
ресторан? First of all, there are different types of places to eat. Let's learn them.

(res-tah-rahn) **ресторан**	= the most expensive and fancy of **русских** restaurants— frequently a dinner-and-dance establishment
(stah-loh-vah-yah) **столовая**	= generally self-service, similar to a cafeteria **или** canteen
(boof-yet) **буфет**	= a snack bar generally found in **гостиницах,** theaters, *(moo-zay-yahk)* **музеях** **и** stations
(bar) **бар**	= exactly that, a place **где** drinks are served
(kahf-yeh) **кафе**	= similar to a restaurant serving meals through the evening

There are some **рестораны** whose names are indicative of the foods they serve.

(shahsh-leech-nah-yah) **шашлычная**	*(shahsh-leek)* = where they serve **шашлык** shashlik, kebabs
(pee-rohzh-kah-vah-yah) **пирожковая**	*(pee-rohzh-kee)* = **где** they serve **пирожки** pastries, small cakes
(bleen-nah-yah) **блинная**	*(blee-nee)* = **где** they serve **блины** pancakes
(pyel-myen-nah-yah) **пельменная**	*(pyel-myen-ee)* = **где они** serve **пельмени** pelmeni, dumplings
(zah-koo-sahch-nah-yah) **закусочная**	*(zah-koo-skee)* = **где они** serve **закуски** snacks

(hah-rah-shee) (res-tah-rahn) *(vhoh-deet-yeh)*
Try them all. Experiment. **Теперь вы** have found **хороший ресторан. Вы входите в**
enter

(nah-hah-deet-yeh) (myes-tah) *(stoh-lih)* *(oh-cheen)*
ресторан и находите место. Sharing **столы с** others is a common **и очень** pleasant
find / seat / tables / very

(ah-bih-chay) *(vee-deet-yeh)* *(stool)*
обычай в СССР. If **вы видите** a vacant **стул,** just be sure to ask
custom / see / chair

(zahn-yah-tah)
Извините. Это место занято?
occupied

(vahm) (noozh-nah)) *(ah-feet-see-ahnt)*
If **вам нужно меню,** catch the attention of **официант и** say
you need / waiter

(die-tee) *(pah-zhahl-yes-tah)*
Официант! Дайте мне меню, пожалуйста.

☐ **февраль** *(fyev-rahl)*.................... February
☐ **фильм** *(feelm)*.................... film
☐ **фотограф** *(fah-toh-grahf)*................ photographer
☐ **Франция** *(frahn-tsee-yah)*................ France
☐ —where they speak **по-французски** *(pah-frahn-tsoo-skee)*

ф

В СССР, there are **три** main meals to enjoy every day, plus **кофе** *(kohf-yeh)* **и** perhaps pastry

(dil-yah)
для the tired traveler late in **днём.** *(dnyohm)*
for   afternoon

(zahv-trahk) **завтрак** =	breakfast … **в СССР** can mean much more than **чай или кофе, хлеб, масло, и** jam. It may include ham **и** **яйца,** *(yight-sah)* **сыр или сосиски.** *(seer)* *(sah-see-skee)* Check serving times eggs cheese sausages before **вы** retire for the night.
(ah-byed) **обед** =	mid-day meal … generally served from 14:00 to 16:00. For most people, this is the main meal of the day.
(oo-zheen) **ужин** =	evening meal … generally served from 19:00 to 22:30; frequently, after 22:30, only cold meals are served.

If **вы** look around you **в русском ресторане, вы** will see that some **русские обычаи** *(ah-bih-chah-ee)* are
customs
different from ours. **Хлеб** *(hlyeb)* may be set directly on the tablecloth, elbows are often rested
bread
на *(nah)* **столе и** please **не** *(nyeh)* forget to mop up your **соус** *(soh-oos)* **с** your **хлебом.** *(hlyeb-ahm)* Before beginning your
sauce
обед, *(ah-byed)* be sure to wish those sharing your table „**Приятного** *(pree-yaht-nah-vah)* **аппетита.**" *(ahp-peh-tee-tah)* If your
enjoy your meal
официант asks if **вы** enjoyed your **обед,** *(ah-byed)* a smile **и** a „**Да, спасибо,**" will tell him that

вы did.

Теперь, it may be breakfast time at home, **но** *(noh)* **вы в СССР и** it is 20:00. Most **русские**
but
рестораны *(res-tah-rah-nee)* post **меню** outside **или** inside. Ask to see **меню** before being seated so **вы**

знаете *(znah-yet-yeh)* what type of **обеды** *(ah-byed-ee)* **и цены** *(tsyen-ee)* **вы** will encounter inside. Most **рестораны** offer a
know   meals   prices
special meal of the day. This is a complete **обед** *(ah-byed)* at a fair **цене.** *(tsyen-yeh)* Be forewarned that
meal   price
frequently all items **в меню** are **не** available. So have a second **и** third choice in mind.

In addition, there are the following main categories **в меню.**

☐ **фрукт** *(frookt)*.....................	fruit		
☐ **футбол** *(foot-bohl)*.................	soccer, football	**Ц**	_____
☐ **царь** *(tsar)*........................	czar, tsar		_____
☐ **цирк** *(tseerk)*.....................	circus		_____
☐ **Чили** *(chee-lee)*...................	Chile	**Ч**	_____

(zah-koos-kee)
закуски . . . . appetizers

(soop)
суп . . . . soup

(yight-sah)
яйца . . . . eggs

(rib-ah)
рыба . . . . fish dishes

(myah-sah)
мясо . . . . meat dishes

(pteet-sah) (deech)
птица и дичь . . . . poultry and game

(oh-vahsh-chee)
овощи . . . . vegetables

(sah-laht)
салат . . . . salad

(dyes-yairt)
десерт . . . . dessert

(slahd-kah-yeh) (bloo-dah)
сладкое   блюдо . . . . sweets

(frook-tih) (seer)
фрукты или сыр . . . . fruit or cheese

(pee-rohzh-nee-yeh)
пирожные . . . . pastries, small cakes

(nah-peet-kee)
напитки . . . . beverages

Most **рестораны** have standard **меню**. Don't expect to get a separate wine list—it is

usually printed on **меню**. Service can be slow, so be prepared to wait between courses.

Теперь for a preview of delights to come... At the back of this *(kuh-nee-gee)* **книги,** **вы** will find a

sample **русское меню**. Read **меню** *(see-vohd-nyah)* **сегодня** и learn **новые слова!** **Когда вы** are ready to
today

leave for **СССР** cut out **меню,** fold it **и** carry it in your pocket, wallet **или** purse. **Не** study

меню until after **вы** have eaten **или вы** will be **очень** hungry.

☐ **шарф** *(sharf)* . . . . scarf
☐ **Швеция** *(shvet-see-yah)* . . . . Sweden
☐ —where they speak **по-шведски** *(pah-shved-skee)*
☐ **штат** *(shtaht)* . . . . state
80 ☐ **шторм** *(shtorm)* . . . . storm

Ш

In addition, learning the following should help you to identify what kind of meat **или**

(hah-teet-yeh) *(zah-kah-zih-vaht)*
poultry **вы хотите** **заказывать** **и как** it will be prepared.
to order

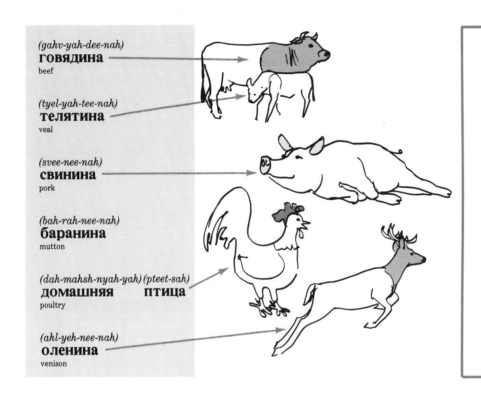

(gahv-yah-dee-nah)
говядина
beef

(tyel-yah-tee-nah)
телятина
veal

(svee-nee-nah)
свинина
pork

(bah-rah-nee-nah)
баранина
mutton

(dah-mahsh-nyah-yah) *(pteet-sah)*
домашняя **птица**
poultry

(ahl-yeh-nee-nah)
оленина
venison

(aht-var-noh-yeh)
отварное = boiled

(zhar-yen-ah-yeh)
жареное = roasted/fried

(toosh-yoh-nah-yeh)
тушёное = stewed

(zahp-yeh-chen-nah-yeh)
запеченное = baked

(nah-too-rahl-nee)
натуральный = grilled

(far-shee-roh-vah-nee)
фаршированый = stuffed

(oh-vahsh-chee) *(ahb-yed-ahm)*
Вы will also get **овощи** with your **обедом** **и** perhaps **салат.** One day at an open-air
vegetables meal

(rin-kyeh) *(nahz-vah-nee-yah)* *(ah-vah-shay)* *(frook-tohv)*
рынке will teach you **названия** for all the different kinds of **овощей и фруктов,** plus it
market names fruit

(mohzh-yet-yeh)
will be a delightful experience for you. **Вы можете** always consult your menu guide at the

(kuh-nee-gee) *(hah-teet-yeh)*
back of **книги** if **вы** forget the correct **название. Теперь вы** have decided what **вы хотите**
would like

(yest) *(ah-feet-see-ahnt)*
есть и официант arrives.
to eat

Я хочу суп и свинину.

Что вы хотите пить?

Стакан белого вина, пожалуйста.

Не forget to treat yourself to **русским десертом.** You would not want to miss out on trying the following **десерт.**

> *(kees-yel)*
> **кисель**
> jello-type dessert
>
> *(mah-roh-zhen-ah-yeh)*
> **мороженое**
> ice cream
>
> *(pee-rohg)*
> **пирог**
> tart
>
> *(roh-mah-vah-yah) (bah-bah)*
> **ромовая баба**
> cake steeped in rum

After completing your **обед,** *(ah-byed)* call **официанта** *(ah-feet-see-ahn-tah)* **и** pay just as **вы** have already learned in Step 16:

> *(die-tee)* *(pah-zhahl-yes-tah)*
> **Дайте счёт, пожалуйста.**

Внизу is a sample **меню** to help you prepare for your holiday.

РЕСТОРАН „ЛЕНИНГРАД"

ОБЕДЕННОЕ МЕНЮ

ГОРЯЧИЕ БЛЮДА
Бефстроганов (beef Stroganoff)................3-77
Котлеты „Ленинградские" (lamb chops)........2-60
Судак в белом вине (perch in white wine).......2-85
Осетрина жареная с помидорами (fried sturgeon
  with tomatoes)...........................2-91
Курица жареная с грибами (fried chicken with
  mushrooms)..............................2-65

ХОЛОДНЫЕ ЗАКУСКИ
Икра (caviar)...........................руб. 5-85
Салат мясной (meat salad)................1-35
Салат с крабами (crab salad)..................1-10
Осетрина (sturgeon)........................1-10

СЛАДКИИ БЛЮДА
Компот из свежих абрикос (compote of fresh
  apricots)..................................-65
Лимонный мусс (lemon mousse)................-85
Мороженое из ягод (berry ice cream)...........-95
Кисель с мороженым (jello with ice cream).......-85

СУПЫ
Борщ украинский............................-45
Щи (cabbage soup)..........................-51
Грибной суп (mushroom soup).................-56
Уха (fish soup)...............................-61

НАПИТКИ
Чай (tea)..................................-20
Кофе (coffee).................................-22
Белое вино (white wine)......................-90
Красное вино (red wine).......................-90
Пиво (beer)..................................-85
Молоко (milk)................................-50
Лимонад (lemonade)..........................-45

САЛАТЫ
Салат из помидоров (tomato salad).............-52
Салат из огурцов (cucumber salad).............-49
Салат из капусты с яблоками(cabbage-and-apple
  salad)....................................-59

Ресторан работает с 9 час. до 23 час. 30

☐ **эскалатор** *(es-kah-lah-tor)*................ escalator
☐ **январь** *(yahn-var)*....................... January
☐ **Япония** *(yah-pohn-ee-yah)*................ Japan
☐ —where they speak **по-японски** *(pah-yah-pohn-skee)*
☐ **яхта** *(yahk-tah)*........................... yacht

Я

(zahv-trahk)
Завтрак is a little different because it can vary from a light continental breakfast to a
breakfast

hearty breakfast of eggs **или** cold cuts **или** vegetables. **Внизу** is a sample of what **вы**

(mohzh-yet-yeh)   *(oo-trahm)*
можете expect to greet you **утром.**
                           in morning

СТОЛОВАЯ „ОКТЯБРЬСКАЯ"

Доброе Утро!

Яйца		**Мясо**	
омлет с сыром	-85	сосиски	-90
cheese		small sausages	
взбитая яичница	-69	колбаса	-89
scrambled eggs		sausage	
яичнийа-глазунья	-59	ветчина жареная	-93
eggs fried		ham fried	

Напитки

чай с лимоном .... -20

чай с вареньем .... -20

кофе чёрный .... -20

кофе с молоком .... -20

апельсиновый сок .... -30
orange   juice

какао .... -20

И...

сыр .... -35
cheese

пирожные .... -28

булочки .... -15
rolls

масло .... -03

варенье .... -02

блинчики с вареньем............ -85

Вот a few special greetings **по-русски.**
☐ **С Рождеством Христовым!** *(rahzh-dyest-vohm hrees-toh-vim)*................Merry Christmas!
☐ **С Новым Годом!** *(noh-vim goh-dahm)* ....Happy New Year!
☐ **С Днём Рождения!** *(dnyohm rahzh-dyen-ee-yah)* ....Happy Birthday!
☐ **Поздравления!** *(pahz-drahv-lyen-ee-yah)* ....Congratulations!

Step 19

(teh-leh-fohn)
Телефон
telephone

What is different about **телефоне в СССР?** *(teh-leh-fohn-yeh)* Well, **вы** never notice such things until **вы**

want to use them. Be warned **теперь** that **телефоны в СССР** *(teh-leh-foh-nee)* are much less numerous

than **в США** *(shah)* **или в Канаде.** Nevertheless, **телефон** allows you to call **друзьям,** *(drooz-yahm)* reserve
friends

билеты *(beel-yet-tee)* **в театр,** *(tee-ah-ter)* **на балет** *(bahl-yet)* **и концерт,** *(kohn-tsairt)* make emergency calls, check on the hours of a

музея, *(moo-zyeh-yah)* rent **машину** *(mah-shee-noo)* **и** all those other things which **нам** *(nahm)* **нужно** *(noozh-nah)* **сделать** on a daily basis.
car   we need   to do

It also gives you a certain amount of freedom **когда вы можете** *(mohzh-yet-yeh)* **позвонить** *(pahz-vah-neet)* on your own.
phone

Having **телефон в гостинице не** as common **в СССР** as **в США.** That means that

вам *(vahm)* **нужно** *(noozh-nah)* **знать** *(znaht)* **как** to find **телефон: на почте,** *(poach-teh)* **на** *(nah)* **улице,** *(oo-leet-seh)* **в баре** *(bar-yeh)* **и** in the lobby of
to know   street   bar

гостиницы.

Вот русский телефон-автомат.

So far, so good. **Теперь,** let's read the
instructions for using **телефон.** This is one
of those moments when you realize,

**Я не в США.
Я не в Канаде.
Я не в Англии.**

So let's learn how to operate **телефон.**

(een-strook-tsee-ee)
Инструкции look complicated but actually are not—some of these **слова вы** should be able
instructions

to recognize already. Let's learn the others. **Вот как инструкции** might go.
(een-strook-tsee-ee)

 ТЕЛЕФОН-АВТОМАТ

1. Pick up the receiver.

2. Drop **две копейки** into the slot.

3. Wait for the dial tone **и** dial **номер.**

These are free telephone calls:

Бесплатно Вызываются

(pah-zhar-nah-yah) *(ah-hrah-nah)* **Пожарная охрана 01** fire	**Скорая помощь 03** emergency medical help
(mee-leet-see-yah) **Милиция 02** police	**Служба газа 04** heating gas service

(ahn-glee-skee) **Английский**	*(roos-skee)* **Русский**	*(ahn-glee-skee)* **Английский**	*(roos-skee)* **Русский**
telephone	=	*(teh-leh-fohn)* **телефон**	public telephone booth	=	**телефон- автомат**
to telephone	=	*(pahz-vah-neet)* **позвонить**	telephone book	=	*(teh-leh-fohn-nah-yah)* **телефонная книга**
operator	=	*(teh-leh-fahn-eest)* **телефонист**	telephone conversation	=	*(rahz-gah-vor)* **разговор по телефону**

Вы не можете звонить other cities from **телефон-автомат.** To call another city
can

(poach-too)
вам нужно идти на почту или **звонить телефонисту из гостиницы.**
you need   to go   operator

На почте tell **телефонисту „Мне нужно позвонить в США.“** Do not be surprised if **вы**

have to pay for your call in advance. Sometimes it is even necessary to order your call a

day in advance.

(troob-koo)   *(ahl-loh)*
When answering **телефон, вы** pick up **трубку и** say, **Алло. Это** _____.
                                        receiver   your name

                                                                                  (voht)
When saying goodbye, you say **„До свиданья“** or **„До завтра.“ Вот** some sample
                                                             until   tomorrow

(dee-ah-loh-gee) *(teh-leh-foh-noo)*
диалоги по телефону. Write them in the blanks **внизу.**
dialogues

(yah)   *(pahz-vah-neet)* *(mahs-kohv-skee)* *(oo-nee-vyair-see-tyet)*
Я хочу позвонить в Московский Университет. _____
           to call   Moscow   university

(hah-choo)   *(chee-kah-goh)*
Я хочу позвонить в Чикаго. _____
           to call   Chicago

(bah-ree-soo) *(nohv-gah-rohd-yeh)*
Я хочу позвонить Борису в Новгороде. _____
           Boris   Novgorod

(eh-lyen-yeh)   *(bah-koo)*
Я хочу позвонить Елене в Баку. _____
           Baku

(air-oh-floht)   *(air-oh-por-too)*
Я хочу позвонить в Аэрофлот в Аэропорту. _____

(lohn-dahn)
Я хочу позвонить в Лондон. _____

Где телефон-автомат? _Где телефон-автомат?_
     public telephone

Где телефонная книга? _____
     book

(moy) *(nohm-yair)*
Мой номер 344-21-89. _____
my

(vahsh)   *(pah-zhahl-yes-tah)*
Ваш номер телефона, пожалуйста? _____
your   number   telephone

                                  (ahk-tyah-ber-skah-yah)
Номер телефона гостиницы „Октябрьская,“ пожалуйста? _____
            of hotel

Вот another possible **диалог.** Pay close attention to **слова и как** they are used.

86

(ee-vahn)
Иван: Алло. Это Иван Иванович. Я хочу поговорить с Анной Петровной.
(ee-vah-nah-veech) *(pah-gah-vah-reet)* *(ahn-noy)*
to speak

(syek-ryair-tar)
Секретарь: Одну минуту, пожалуйста. Извините, но линия занята.
one *(lee-nee-yah)* *(zahn-yah-tah)*
line busy

(pahv-tah-reet-yeh) *(mah-lah)*
Иван: Повторите, пожалуйста. Я мало говорю по-русски.
repeat a little

(myed-len-nah)
Говорите медленно.
speak slowly

Секретарь: Извините, но линия занята.

Иван: Ох. Спасибо. До свиданья.

И still another possibility...

(kaht-yah) *(noozh-yen)* *(pee-troh-veech-ah)*
Катя: Мне нужен номер телефона доктора Петровича в Иркутске, пожалуйста.

(teh-leh-fahn-eest) *(nohm-yair)*
Телефонист: Номер 254-43-96.

Катя: Повторите номер, пожалуйста.

Телефонист: Номер 254-43-96.

Катя: Большое спасибо. До свиданья.

Телефонист: Пожалуйста. До свиданья.

(myed-lyen-nah)
Вы теперь ready to use any **телефон в СССР.** Just take it **медленно и** speak clearly.
slowly

(mohzh-yet-yeh)
Не forget that **вы можете** ask...
can

(skohl-kah) *(stoy-eet)* *(pahz-vah-neet)* *(ree-goo)* *(shah)*
Сколько стоит позвонить в Ригу?   Сколько стоит позвонить в США?
to call Riga U.S.A.

————————————————   ————————————————

(kee-yev)
Сколько стоит позвонить в Киев?   Сколько стоит позвонить в Англию?
Kiev

————————————————   ————————————————

(vahm) *(myel-ahch)*
Remember that **вам нужна мелочь для телефона.**
you need change

87

Step 20

(myeh-troh)
Метро
subway

An excellent means of transportation **в СССР** is *(myeh-troh)* **метро.** Both **в Ленинграде** **и** **в**
subway

Москве, метро is an extensive system with express lines to the suburbs. *(trahm-vy)* **Трамвай** is also
streetcar/trolley

a good means of transportation, plus **вы можете** see your surroundings **на** *(trahm-vah-yeh)* **трамвае.**

(kahk-ee-yeh) *(noozh-nee)* *(myeh-troh)* *(trahm-vah-yeh)*
Какаие **слова нужны** **для** a traveler **на метро,** **на автобусе, на трамвае** **или** **в** **такси?**
what kind of   words   necessary   on   subway

Let's learn them by practicing them aloud **и** then by writing them in the blanks below.

(myeh-troh)   *(trahm-vy)*   *(ahv-toh-boos)*
метро   **трамвай**   **автобус**

метро, метро _____ _____

(ahs-tah-nohv-kah)
остановка = stop _____

(ahv-toh-boo-sah)
остановка автобуса = bus stop _____

(lee-nee-yah)
линия = line _____

(kahs-sah)
касса = ticket machine касса, касса, касса

(trahm-vah-yah)
остановка трамвая = trolley stop _____

(stahnt-see-yah)
станция метро = metro station _____

Let's also review the "transportation" verbs at this point. Yes, both *(oo-yez-zhaht)* **„уезжать"** and

(oo-hah-deet)
„уходить" can mean "to leave." Don't worry about it, just be aware of it.

(oo-yez-zhaht)
уезжать = to leave (by vehicle)

(oo-hah-deet)
уходить = to leave (on foot)

_____ _____

(pree-yez-zhaht)
приезжать = to arrive

(pree-hah-deet)
приходить = to arrive

Maps displaying the various **линии** *(lee-nee-ee)* lines **и остановки** *(ahs-tah-nohv-kee)* stops are generally posted inside **станции** *(stahnt-see-ee)* **метро.** Almost every **карта Москвы и Ленинграда** has **метро** map included. **Линии** are color-coded to facilitate reading. **Метро в Москве** has over 50 **станций** *(stahnt-see-ee)* **и** is famous for its elaborate stations with mosaics, chandeliers, paintings **и** sculptures. To enter **метро, вам нужно** to drop **пять копеек** *(pyaht)* into the turnstile at **входа.** *(vhoh-dah)* entrance **Вам нужно** a five-kopeck coin which is commonly called **„пятак.“** Other than having foreign words, the Russian **метро** functions just like **метро в США, в Канаде или в Англии.** Locate your destination, select the correct line **и** hop on board. See **карту внизу.**

The same basic set of **слова и вопросы** will see you through traveling **на метро, на автобусе, на трамвае, на машине и** even **на поезде.**

Naturally, the first **вопрос** is „где."

(stahnt-see-yah)
Где станция Метро?
(ahs-tah-nohv-kah)
Где остановка автобуса?
(trahm-vah-yah)
Где остановка трамвая?
(stah-yahn-kah)
Где стоянка такси?

Practice the following basic **вопросы** out loud **и** then write them in the blanks below.

1. *(stahnt-see-yah)*
    Где станция Метро? _____

    Где остановка автобуса? _____

    Где стоянка такси? Где стоянка такси?

2. *(chahs-tah)(hah-deet)*
    Как часто ходит автобус номер 36? _____
    how   often   goes
    (trahm-vy)
    Как часто ходит трамвай номер 20? _____
    (poh-yezd)
    Как часто ходит поезд? _____
    train

3. *(kahg-dah) (aht-hah-deet)*
    Когда отходит автобус номер восемь? _____
    leaves

    Когда отходит трамвай номер три? _____
    (tsen-ter)
    Когда отходит поезд в центр? _____
    city center

4. *(ee-dyoht)*
    Идёт автобус до Большого Театра? _____

    Идёт трамвай до Зоопарка? _____

    Идёт поезд до Гостиницы Метрополь? _____

5. **Сколько стоит билет на Метро?** _____

    Сколько стоит билет на автобус? _____

    Сколько стоит билет на поезд? Сколько стоит билет на поезд?

    Сколько стоит билет на трамвай? _____

Теперь that **вы** have gotten into the swing of things, practice the following patterns aloud

90 substituting „автобус" for „метро" and so on.

1. *(mah-goo)*
   Где я могу купить билет на Метро? На автобус? На поезд?
   can buy

2. *(aht-hah-deet)*   *(oo-nee-vyair-see-tyet)*
   Когда отходит поезд в Университет? В Гостиницу Ленинград? В Аэропорт?
   leaves   university

   (tsen-ter)   *(moo-zay)*
   В Зоопарк? В Центр? В Театр? В Музей Ленина?
            city center

3. *(stahnt-see-yah)*
   Где станция метро „Проспект Маркса"?

   Где станция метро „Библиотека Ленина"?

   (ahs-tah-nohv-kah)
   Где остановка автобуса номер 17?

   Где остановка трамвая номер 11?

   Где станция метро „Университет"?

   Где станция метро „Аэропорт"?

   Где остановка автобуса восемь?

   Где станция метро „Вокзал"?

М

УНИВЕРСИТЕТ
АЭРОПОРТ
ЗООПАРК
МУЗЕЙ ЛЕНИНА
ЦЕНТР
ВОКЗАЛ

Read the following very typical conversation и write it in the blanks направо.

(kah-tor-ah-yah)   *(dil-yah)(oo-nee-vyair-see-tyet-ah)*
Которая линия для университета? _____
which
(krahs-nah-yah)
Красная линия до университета. _____
red
(chahs-tah)
Как часто? _____
how often
(kahzh-dee-yeh)
Каждые пять минут. _Каждые пять минут._
every
(men-yeh) (noozh-nah) (sdyeh-laht) (pyair-yeh-sahd-koo)
Мне нужно сделать пересадку? _____
do I need to make transfer
(vahm)   *(sdyeh-laht) (pyair-yeh-sahd-koo)*
Да, у зоопарка вам нужно сделать пересадку. _____
          you need
(skohl-kah) (vreh-mee-nee)
Сколько времени занимает до университета? _____
how much time takes

Двадцать минут. _____

Сколько стоит билет до университета? _____

(kah-pyeh-eek)
Пять копеек. _____

91

Вы можете translate the following thoughts **на русский? Ответы внизу.**

1. Where is the subway station? _____

2. What does a ticket cost to the university? _____

3. How often goes the bus to the airport? _____

4. Where can I buy a ticket for the subway? _____

5. Where is the bus stop? _____

6. Where is the exit? _____

7. Do I need to transfer?_____

8. Where do I need to transfer? _____

Here are **три** more verbs.

(stee-raht)
стирать = to wash/clean (clothes)

(tyair-yaht)
терять = to lose

(zah-nee-mah-yet)
занимает = it takes

стирать _____ _____

Вы знаете the basic "plug-in" formula, so translate the following thoughts **с** these new verbs. **Ответы тоже внизу.**

1. I wash the jacket. _____

2. You wash the clothes._____

3. It takes 20 minutes to go to the Kremlin. _____

4. By car it takes three hours to Odessa._____

(prah-dah-vaht) *(pah-koo-paht)*
Продавать и Покупать
to sell   to buy

Shopping abroad is exciting. The simple everyday task of buying *(lee-ter)* **литр** *(mah-lah-kah)* **молока или**
                                                                   liter   milk

(yah-blah-kah)   *(vwee)*
яблоко becomes a challenge that **вы** should **теперь** be able to meet quickly **и** easily.
apple

(soov-yen-ee-ree)   *(nyeh)*
Of course, **вы** will purchase **сувениры, марки и открытки,** but **не** forget those many other
                    souvenirs

(vesh-chee)   *(znah-yet-yeh)*
вещи ranging from shoelaces to **аспирина** that **вы** might need unexpectedly. **Вы знаете**
things   do you know

(myezh-doo) *(kuh-neezh-nim)* *(mah-gah-zee-nahm)*
the difference **между** <u>**книжным магазином**</u> **и** <u>**почтой**</u>? **Нет.** Let's learn about the
                     ¦ between   book   store

(aht-dyel-ahk)
different **отделах и магазинах в СССР. Внизу карта** of a section of **Москвы.**
      shops   stores

(mah-gah-zeen)
На the following **странице,** there are all types of **магазин вы** might find **в СССР.**
on

Be sure to fill in the blanks **под** *(kar-teen-kah-mee)* **картинками** с *(nahz-vah-nee-yah-mee)* **названиями магазинов.**
                          under   names

(boo-lahch-nah-yah)
булочная, где
bakery
(koo-peet) *(hlyeb)*
можно купить хлеб
one can   buy   bread

(myahs-noy) *(mah-gah-zeen)*
мясной магазин, где
butcher   shop
(mohzh-nah) *(myah-sah)*
можно купить мясо
meat

(prahch-yech-nah-yah)
прачечная, где
laundry
(stee-raht) *(ah-dyezh-doo)*
можно стирать одежду
wash   clothes

(kahf-yeh)
кафе, где
cafe
(peet)
можно пить кофе
drink

(skahb-yah-noy) *(mah-gah-zeen)*
скобяной магазин, где
hardware   store
(bah-tar-yeh-yoo)
можно купить батарею
battery

(ahp-tyek-ah)
аптека, где
pharmacy
(ahs-pee-reen)
можно купить аспирин
aspirin

(tsveh-tohch-nih)
цветочный магазин,
flower   shop

где можно купить

(tsvet-ee)
цветы

(tah-bahch-nih)
табачный магазин,
tobacco   store

где можно купить

(see-gar-yet-tih)
табак и сигареты
cigarettes

(kahn-deet-yair-skah-yah)
кондитерская, где
candy store
(kahn-fyet-tih)
можно купить конфеты
candy

(shah-kah-lahd)
и шоколад
chocolate

(mah-lohch-nah-yah)
молочная, где
dairy

(mah-lah-koh)
можно купить молоко
milk

(bool-lahch-nah-yah)
булочная, где
pastry shop

(mohzh-nah) *(pryah-nee-kee)*
можно купить пряники
pastries

(oh-vahsh-chnoy) *(mah-gah-zeen)*
овощной магазин, где
greengrocer's

(oh-vahsh-chee)
можно купить овощи
vegetables

МОЛОЧНАЯ

БУЛОЧНАЯ

ОВОЩНОЙ МАГАЗИН

(stah-yahn-kah)
стоянка, где
parking lot

(stah-veet)
можно ставить
park/put

(mah-shee-noo)
машину
car

(pah-reek-mahk-yairs-kah-yah)
парикмахерская,
hairdresser

(stree-goot)
где стригут
cut

(voh-lah-see)
волосы
hair

(ah-tyel-yeh)
ателье, где
tailor

(part-noy) *(shyoht)*
портной шьёт
tailor   sews

(ah-dyezh-doo)
одежду
clothes

СТОЯНКА

ПАРИКМАХЕРСКАЯ

АТЕЛЬЕ

ателье

(poach-tah)
почта, где
post office

можно купить

марки

(aht-dyel-yen-yeh) *(mee-leet-see)*
отделение милиции,
police station

(ny-tee)
где можно найти
find

(mee-leet-see-yoo)
милицию
police

(bahnk)
банк, где
bank

(ahb-myen-yaht)
можно обменять
exchange

(dyen-gee)
деньги
money

ПОЧТА

ОТДЕЛЕНИЕ МИЛИЦИИ

БАНК

(prahd-mahg)
продмаг, где
food store
(myah-sah)
можно купить мясо,
meat
(frook-tee) *(mah-lah-koh)*
фрукты и молоко

(gah-strah-nohm)
гастроном, где
delicatessen
можно купить
(kahl-bah-soo)
колбасу
sausage

(bair-yohz-kah)
„Берёзка," где
specialty store
(vwee) *(moh-zhet-yeh)*
вы можете купить
(mah-trohsh-kee) *(yahn-tar)*
матрёшки и янтарь
Russian dolls   amber

ПРОДМАГ

ГАСТРОНОМ

БЕРЁЗКА

(kee-noh)
кино, где
cinema
(pahs-maht-rairt)
можно посмотреть
see
(feelm)
фильм
film

КИНО

КИНО, КИНО

(kee-ohsk)
киоск, где
newsstand
можно купить
(gah-zyet-ee) *(zhoor-nahl-ee)*
газеты и журналы

КИОСК

(heem-cheest-kah)
химчистка, где
dry cleaner's
(cheest-yaht) *(ah-dyezh-doo)*
чистят одежду
clean   clothes
(hee-mee-ches-kee)
химически
chemically

ХИМЧИСТКА

(kahnt-stah-vah-ree)
канцтовары, где
stationery store
(rooch-kee)
можно купить ручки,
pens
(boo-mah-goo) *(kah-rahn-dah-shee)*
бумагу и карандаши
paper   pencils

(kuh-neezh-nee)
книжный магазин,
bookstore
где можно купить
(kuh-nee-gee)
книги
books

(oo-nee-vyair-mahg)
универмаг, где
department store
(vsyoh)
можно купить всё
everything

(see Step 22)

КАНЦТОВАРЫ

КНИЖНЫЙ МАГАЗИН

УНИВЕРМАГ

(rin-ahk)
рынок, где
market

можно купить

фрукты и овощи

(foh-toh-mah-gah-zeen)
фотомагазин,
camera supplies

где можно купить

(foh-toh-plohn-kee)
фотоплёнки
film

(ahv-tah-stahnt-see-yah)
автостанция,
service station

где можно купить

(byen-zeen)
бензин
gas/petrol

ФОТОМАГАЗИН

(byoo-roh) (poot-yeh-shest-vee)
бюро путешествий
travel agency

где можно купить

(sah-mahl-yoht)
билеты на самолёт

(chah-see)
часы, где

можно купить

часы

(rib-nee) (rin-ahk)
рыбный рынок,
fish market

где можно

(rib-oo)
купить рыбу

БЮРО ПУТЕШЕСТВИЙ — ЧАСЫ — РЫБНЫЙ РЫНОК

(aht-krih-tee) *(dnyohm)*
Магазины are generally **открыты с 8-ми до 20-ти часов. Днём с 13-ти до 14-ти**
open

(zah-krih-tee) *(gah-strah-nohm)*
магазины закрыты for lunch. To make one stop for food, go to a „**гастроном.**" Within
closed

(aht-dyel-ee) *(hlyeb-nee)* *(kahn-deet-yair-skee)* *(mah-lohch-nee)* *(myahs-noy)*
this store **вы** will find many small **отделы: хлебный, кондитерский, молочный, мясной**
shops

(frook-toh-vee)
и фруктовый. В гастрономе вы не можете купить овощей. Овощи are sold **на рынках.**
markets

Is there anything else which **вы** will want to know about Russian stores? **Да.** Look at

картинку на next **странице.**

97

4. четвёртый этаж *(eh-tahzh)*

3. третий этаж

2. второй этаж

1. первый этаж

While **в Москве вы** will probably want to visit **ГУМ,** *(goom)* short for „**Государственный** *(gah-soo-darst-vyen-nee)*

(oo-nee-vyair-sahl-nee)
Универсальный Магазин." ГУМ sells everything **от чемоданов до телевизоров.**

Теперь вы know the names for **русских магазином,** let's practice shopping.

1. First step—**Где?**

Где молочная? **Где банк?** **Где кино?**

Go through **магазины** introduced in this Step **и** ask, „**где**" with each **магазине.**

(boo-lahch-nah-yah)
Где булочная?

(prahch-yech-nah-yah)
Где прачечная?

Где кафе?

(ahp-tyek-ah)
Где аптека?

II. Next step—tell them what **вы** are looking for, need **или хотите!**

1) **Мне нужно…** _____

2) **У вас есть…?** _____
do you have

3) **Я хочу…** Я хочу _____

(men-yeh)　　　　　*(kah-rahn-dahsh)*
Мне нужно купить карандаш.

(oo) (vahs) (yest)
У вас есть карандаш?
do you have

Я хочу купить карандаш.

(kee-loh) (yah-blahk)
Мне нужно кило яблок?
　　　　　　kilo　　apples

У вас есть кило яблок?
　　　　　　　　　apples

Я хочу купить кило яблок.

Go through the glossary at the end of *(et-toy)* **этой** **книги и** select *(dvahd-tset)* **двадцать слов.** Drill the above
　　　　　　　　　　　　　　　　　　this

patterns **с** *(et-tee-mee)* **этими двадцатью словами.** Don't cheat. Drill them *(see-vohd-nyah)* **сегодня. Теперь,** take

(dvahd-tset)
двадцать more **слов из** your glossary **и** do the same.

III. Next step—find out *(skohl-kah)* **сколько** *(et-tah)* **это** *(stoy-eet)* **стоит.**

Сколько это стоит? _____

Сколько стоит карандаш?

(aht-krit-kah)
Сколько стоит открытка?

Сколько стоит марка?

Сколько стоит карта?
　　　　　　map

Сколько стоит кило яблок?

(ah-pyel-see-nahv)
Сколько стоит кило апельсинов?
　　　　　　　　　　oranges
　　　　　　　　　　(myah-sah)
Сколько стоит кило мяса?
　　　　　　　　　　meat
　　　　　　　　　(chahsh-kah)
Сколько стоит чашка чая?
　　　　　　　　cup　　tea

Using these same **слова** that **вы** selected above, drill **эти вопросы тоже.**
　　　　　　　　　　　　　　　　　　　　　　　these

IV. If **вы не** *(znah-yet-yeh)* **знаете где** to find something, **вы можете** *(sprah-seet)* **спросить**
　　　　　　　　know　　　　　　　　　　　　　　　　　　　　　　　　ask

(mah-goo)
Где я могу купить аспирин?

(ahch-kee)
Где я могу купить очки?

Once **вы** find what **вы** would like, **говорите,** *(gah-vah-reet-yeh)*
　　　　　　　　　　　　　　　　　　say

Я хочу это, пожалуйста.

Или if **вы** would not like it,

(et-tah-vah)
Я не хочу этого, спасибо.
　　　　　　　　　that

Теперь, вы are all set to shop for anything!

(oo-nee-vyair-sahl-nee)   (mah-gah-zeen)

Универсальный Магазин
department   store

At this point, **вы** should just about be ready for your **поездки в СССР. Вы** have gone
trip

shopping for those last-minute odds 'n ends. Most likely, the store directory at your local

(oo-nee-vyair-sahl-nee)
универсальный магазин did not look like the one **внизу. Вы** already know **много слов и**
department   store

вы можете guess at **много** others. **Вы знаете что** _(zhen-shchee-nah)_ „**женщина**" is Russian for "woman"

so if **вам нужно** something for a woman, **вы** would probably look **на** _(vtah-rahm)_ _(eh-tahzh-yeh)_ **втором этаже,**
                                                            second   floor

wouldn't you?

7. этаж	Булочная Кафе Спиртной напиток	Вино Фрукты Овоши Мясо	Дичь Пища Домашняя пища Мороженая пища
6. этаж	Кровати Полотно Зеркала	Мебель Лампы Ковры	Картины Электроприборы
5. этаж	Посуда Хрусталь Фарфор	Ножевые изделия Кухонные приборы	Ключи Керамика
4. этаж	Книги Телевизоры Игрушки Радио	Табак Газеты Журналы Ресторан	Детская мебель Музыкальные инструменты Писчебумажный отдел Пластнки
3. этаж	Косметика Бельё Платки	Детский отдел Детские туфли Купальные костюмы	Антикварные вещи Фотографические аппараты
2. этаж	Женская одежда Женские шляпы Женские туфли	Мужская одежда Мужские шляпы Мужские туфли	Носки Пояса Зонтики

1. этаж	Духи
	Конфеты
	Часы
	Перчатки
		Кожаные вещи
		Юверлирные изделия
		Рабочие инструменты
		Спортивные
		  принадлежности
			Части автомобиля
			Принадлежности
			  туалета
			Карты

(ah-dyezh-dee)
Let's start a checklist **для поездки.** Besides **одежды, что вам нужно?**
trip

(pahs-port)
паспорт

(beel-yet)
билет

(cheh-mah-dahn)
чемодан

чемодан ✓

(soom-kah)
сумка

(boo-mahzh-neek)
бумажник

(dyen-gee)
деньги

(foh-toh-ahp-pah-raht)
фотоаппарат

(foh-toh-plohn-kah)
фотоплёнка

Take the next **восемь** labels и label *(et-tee)* **эти вещи** *(seh-vohd-nyah)* **сегодня.** Better yet, assemble them **в углу**

of your **дома.**

(poot-yeh-shest-voo-yet-yeh) *(zee-moy)* *(lyet-ahm)*
Вы путешествуете   в СССР зимой или летом? Не forget…

(koo-pahl-nee) *(kahst-yoom)*
купальный костюм
swimsuit

(sahn-dahl-ee-ee)
сандалии
sandals

Не forget the basic toiletries either!

(mwee-lah)
мыло
soap

мыло ✓

(zoob-nah-yah) (shyoht-kah)
зубная   щётка
toothbrush

(zoob-nah-yah) (pahs-tah)
зубная   паста
toothpaste

(breet-vah)
бритва
razor

(dyeh-zah-dah-rah-tor)
дезодоратор
deodorant

(gryeb-yen)
гребень
comb

101

For the rest of **вещи** let's start with the outside layers **и** work our way in.

(pahl-toh)
пальто
overcoat

_____ ☑

(plahshch)
плащ
raincoat

_____ ☐

(zohn-teek)
зонтик
umbrella

_____ ☐

(pyair-chaht-kee)
перчатки
gloves

_____ ☐

(shlah-pah)
шляпа
hat

_____ ☐

(sah-pah-gee)
сапоги
boots

_____ ☐

(too-flee)
туфли
shoes

_____ ☐

(nahs-kee)
носки
socks

НОСКИ ☑

(chool-kee)
чулки
stockings

_____ ☐

Take the next **пятнадцать** labels **и** label **эти вещи.** *(et-tee)* / these. Check **и** make sure that **они чистые и** *(chees-tih-yeh)* / clean

ready **для поездки.** *(pah-yezd-kee)* / trip. Be sure to do the same **с** the rest of **вещами** *(vesh-shah-mee)* that **вы** pack. Check them

off on this list as **вы** organize them. From now on, **у вас** *(oo) (vahs)* / you have „зубная паста" *(zoob-nah-yah) (pahs-tah)* **и не**

"toothpaste."

(pee-zhah-mah)
пижама

_____ ☐

(nahch-nah-yah)(roo-bahsh-kah)
ночная рубашка

_____ ☐

(koo-pahl-nee) (hah-laht)
купальный халат
bathrobe

_____ ☐

(bahsh-mah-kee)
башмаки
slippers

_____ ☐

(koo-pahl-nee) *(hah-laht)* *(bahsh-mah-kee)* *(moh-goot)* *(vahs)* *(plyah-zheh)*
Купальный халат и башмаки могут double **для вас на пляже.**
can / you / at / beach

102

(kahst-yoom)
костюм
suit

(gahl-stook)
галстук
tie

plah-tohk)
платок
handkerchief

(roo-bahsh-kah)
рубашка
shirt

(peed-zhahk)
пиджак
jacket/blazer

(bryoo-kee)
брюки
trousers

(plaht-yeh)
платье
dress

(blooz-kah)
блузка
blouse

(yoob-kah)
юбка
skirt

(sveet-yair)
свитер
sweater

(leef-cheek)
лифчик
brassiere

(kahm-bee-nahsh-kah)
комбинашка
slip

(troo-sih)
трусы
underpants

(my-kah)
майка
undershirt

_____ ☐

_____ ☐

_____ ☐

_____ ☐

_____ ☐

брюки ✓

_____ ☐

_____ ☐

_____ ☐

_____ ☐

_____ ☐

_____ ☐

(et-tee)   *(pah-yek-haht)*
Having assembled **эти вещи, вы** are ready **поехать.** However, being human means
        these   to go

(oo-nee-vyair-sahl-nee)
occasionally forgetting something. Look again **в универсальный магазин** directory.

(kah-kohm) (eh-tahzh-yeh)   *(ny-tee)*
На каком этаже можно найти...
which   floor   can one   find

(moozh-koo-yoo) (ah-dyezh-doo)
мужкую одежду?   На ___ВТОРОМ___ *(eh-tahzh-yeh)* **этаже.**

(zhen-skoo-yoo)
женскую одежду?   На _____ **этаже.**
women's   clothing

книги?   На _____ **этаже.**

(byel-yoh)
бельё?   На _____ **этаже.**
lingerie

103

(hroos-tahl)
хрусталь?
crystal

На _____ этаже.

(doo-hee)
духи?
perfume

На _____ этаже.

(ee-groosh-kee)
игрушки?

На _____ этаже.

Теперь, just remember your basic **вопросы.** *(pahv-tah-reet-yeh)* *(dee-ah-lohg)* **Повторите диалог внизу** out loud **и** then
repeat

by filling in the blanks.

(ny-tee) *(zhyen-skee-yeh)* *(bryoo-kee)*
Где можно найти женские брюки? _____
can one   find   women's   trousers

В женской одежде. _____
clothing
(ah-dyezh-dah)
Где женская одежда? _____

(vtah-rahm)
На втором этаже. На втором этаже.
second

(ny-tee) *(mih-lah)*
Где можно найти мыло и зубню пасту?_____
find   soap
(pyair-vahm)
На первом этаже. _____
first

Also, **не** forget **спросить...** *(sprah-seet)*
to ask

(leeft)
Где лифт? _____
elevator
(lyest-neet-sah)
Где лестница? _____
stair
(es-kah-lah-tar)
Где эскалатор?_____
escalator

(vahm) *(zhyen-skee-yeh)* *(bryoo-kee)* *(moozh-koo-yoo)* *(roo-bahsh-koo)*
Whether **вам нужно купить женские брюки или мужкую рубашку,** the necessary
you   need

слова the same. **Где брюки? Где блузка?**

(kah-tor-ee) *(rahz-myair)*
Который размер?
what   size

_____

(too-fel)
Который размер туфель?
         size   shoes

_____

(hah-rah-shoh) *(see-deet)*
Хорошо сидит.
well   it fits

Хорошо сидит.

_____

(ploh-hah) *(see-deet)*
Плохо сидит
badly   it fits

_____

Я хочу купить это.

_____

Сколько это стоит?

_____

(vsyoh)
Это всё, большое спасибо.
that's   all

_____

Clothing Sizes: *(zhen-shchee-nee)* **ЖЕНЩИНЫ**

Туфли									
American/British	32	34	36	38	40	42	44		
Russian	40	42	44	46	48	50	52		

Одежда									
American	8	10	12	14	16	18			
British	30	32	34	36	38	40			
Russian	36	38	40	42	44	46			

Блузки, Свитеры									
American	5	5½	6	6½	7	7½	8	8½	9
Continental	35	35	36	37	37	38	38½	39	40

Clothing Sizes: *(moozh-chee-nee)* **МУЖЧИНЫ**

Туфли									
American/British	7	7½	8	8½	9	9½	10	10½	11	11½
Russian	41	42	42	43	43	44	44	44	45	45

Одежда								
American/British	34	36	38	40	42	44	46	48
Russian	44	46	48	50	52	54	56	58

Рубашки								
American/British	14	14½	15	15½	16	16½	17	17½
Russian	36	37	38	40	41	42	43	44

(pah-yek-haht)
Теперь вы are ready **поехать.** **Вы знаете** *(znah-yet-yeh)* *(vsyoh)* **всё** that you need. The next Step gives you a
to go   everything

quick review of the Russian alphabet **и** pronunciation **и** then **вы** are off to **аэродром.** *(air-oh-drohm)*

(oo-dah-chee) *(schahst-lee-vah-vah)* *(poo-tee)*
Удачи! Счастливого пути!
     have a good trip

(Continued from page 2)

(sport)
спорт _____
sport

(teh-leh-fohn)
телефон _____
telephone

(tseerk)
цирк _____
circus

(chee-slah)
числа числа
numbers

(shkoh-lah)
школа _____
school

(borsht)
борщ _____
Russian soup/borsch

(et-tah)
это _____
this/that

(myen-yoo)
меню _____
menu

(vahn-nah-yah)
ванная _____
bathroom

There are also four special letters in Russian:

(ee/ih)
ы _____

(chah-see)
часы _____
clock

(sin)
сын _____
son

(varies)
й _____

(moo-zay)
музей _____
museum

(zee-moy)
зимой _____
in winter

ь = *soft sign* **ъ** = *hard sign*	*These two letters do not have a sound. They act as word dividers and affect the preceding letter. So do not try to pronounce them. Here are some examples:*

(skohl-kah)
сколько _____
how much

(spahl-nyah)
спальня _____
bedroom

(shest)
шесть _____
six

Ы Щ Ж Й Д Э Г Ф

(ahl-fah-veet)
Алфавит

Here is the entire Russian alphabet in alphabetical order for quick reference. To make learning the alphabet more fun, practice these new letters and sounds with the examples given, which are Russian names.
A black underline indicates a man's name and a red underline is for a woman's. Once you are finished here, turn to page one and practice saying the geographical locations indicated on the map.

Russian letter	English sound	Example	Write it here
а	ah	**Анна** *(ahn-nah)*	
б	b	**Борис** *(bor-ees)*	
в	v	**Вадим** *(vah-deem)*	
г	g (or v)	**Глеб** *(gleb)*	Глеб
д	d	**Дмитрий** *(dmee-tree)*	
е *(varies)*	eh *(as in let)*	**Елена** *(eh-lyen-ah)*	
	yeh *(as in yet)*		
ё	yoh	**Пётр** *(pyoh-ter)*	
ж	zh	**Жанна** *(zhahn-nah)*	
з	z	**Зина** *(zee-nah)*	
и	ee	**Никита** *(nee-kee-tah)*	

й *(varies)*	oy/ay/i/ee	**Майя** *(my-yah)*	_____
к	k	**Катя** *(kaht-yah)*	_____
л	l	**Лариса** *(lah-ree-sah)*	_____
м	m	**Максим** *(mahk-seem)*	_____
н	n	**Николай** *(nee-koh-lie)*	_____
о *(varies)*	oh	**Ольга** *(ohl-gah)*	Ольга
	ah	**Полина** *(pah-lee-nah)*	_____
п	p	**Паша** *(pah-shah)*	_____
р	r	**Рина** *(ree-nah)*	_____
с	s	**Сергей** *(syair-gay)*	_____
т	t	**Татьяна** *(taht-yah-nah)*	_____
у	oo	**Эдуард** *(ed-oo-ard)*	_____
ф	f	**Софья** *(sohf-yah)*	_____
х	h (or hk)	**Михаил** *(mee-hah-eel)*	_____
ц	ts	**Царёв** *(tsar-yohv)*	_____
ч	ch	**Вячеслав** *(vyah-cheh-slahv)*	_____
ш	sh	**Саша** *(sah-shah)*	_____
щ *(varies)*	shch/sht/sh	**Щукин** *(shchoo-keen)*	_____
ъ	no sound/called a hard sign		_____
ы *(varies)*	ee/ih	**Рыбаков** *(rih-bah-kahv)*	_____
ь	no sound/called a soft sign		_____
э *(varies)*	eh/air	**Элла** *(el-lah)*	_____
ю	yoo	**Юрий** *(yoor-ee)*	_____
я	yah	**Юлия** *(yool-ee-yah)*	_____

By now you should have a reasonable grasp on the Russian alphabet. Letters can change their pronunciation depending upon whether they are stressed or unstressed. Take the letter **о.** It is pronounced _"oh"_ when stressed and _"ah"_ otherwise. Now that isn't so difficult, is it?

Sometimes the phonetics may seem to contradict your pronunciation guide. Don't panic! The easiest and best possible phonetics have been chosen for each individual word. Pronounce the phonetics just as you see them. Don't over-analyze them. Try to speak with a Russian accent and, above all, enjoy yourself!

GLOSSARY

А

абрикос . . . . apricot
август . . . . August
авиапочта . . . . airmail
авиация . . . . aviation
Австралия . . . . Australia
автобиография . . . . autobiography
автобус . . . . bus
автограф . . . . autograph
автомат . . . . automat
автомобиль . . . . car
автор . . . . author
автостанция . . . . service station
агент . . . . agent
адвокат . . . . advocate, lawyer
адрес . . . . address
Азия . . . . Asia
академия . . . . academy
аккуратный . . . . fastidious, neat
акробат . . . . acrobat
акт . . . . act
актёр . . . . actor
акцент . . . . accent
алгебра . . . . algebra
алкоголь . . . . alcohol
алло . . . . hello
Америка . . . . America
Англия . . . . England
по-английски . . . . in English
анекдот . . . . anecdote, joke
антенна . . . . antenna
антибиотики . . . . antibiotics
апельсин . . . . orange (fruit)
аппетит . . . . appetite
апрель . . . . April
аптека . . . . drugstore
арена . . . . arena
арест . . . . arrest
армия . . . . army
аспирин . . . . aspirin
астронавт . . . . astronaut
ателье . . . . tailor's
атлет . . . . athlete
аэродром, аэропорт . . . . airport

Б

бабушка . . . . grandmother
багаж . . . . baggage
базар . . . . bazaar
бал . . . . ball (dance)
балалайка . . . . balalaika
балерина . . . . ballerina
балет . . . . ballet
балкон . . . . balcony
банан . . . . banana
банк . . . . bank
бар . . . . bar (restaurant)
баранина . . . . mutton
баржа . . . . barge
барьер . . . . barrier
бас . . . . bass (voice)

баскетбол . . . . basketball
батарея . . . . battery
башмаки . . . . slippers
беден . . . . poor
без . . . . minus, without
белый . . . . white
бензин . . . . gas/petrol
„Берёзка" . . . . specialty store
билет . . . . ticket
бинокль . . . . binoculars
бланк . . . . blank (form)
богат . . . . rich
бокс . . . . boxing
болен . . . . sick
большой . . . . big, large
больше . . . . more
бомба . . . . bomb
борщ . . . . borsch (beet soup)
брат . . . . brother
брать . . . . to take
бритва . . . . razor
бронза . . . . bronze
брюнет . . . . brunette (male)
будет . . . . will be
будильник . . . . alarm clock
булочная . . . . bakery, pastry shop
бульвар . . . . boulevard
бумага . . . . paper
бумажник . . . . wallet
бюро . . . . bureau, office
был . . . . was
быстро . . . . fast

В

в . . . . in
важно . . . . important
ваза . . . . vase
вальс . . . . waltz
вам нужно . . . . you need
ванная . . . . bathroom
ваша . . . . your
веранда . . . . veranda
весной . . . . in spring
ветрено . . . . windy
вечер . . . . evening
вещи . . . . things
видеть . . . . to see
вилка . . . . fork
вино . . . . wine
витамин . . . . vitamin
внизу . . . . downstairs/below
вода . . . . water
водка . . . . vodka
вокзал . . . . train station
волейбол . . . . volleyball
вопрос . . . . question
восемь . . . . eight
восемнадцать . . . . eighteen
восемьдесят . . . . eighty
восемьсот 800
воскресенье . . . . Sunday
восток . . . . east
восточный . . . . eastern
вот . . . . here is

врач . . . . doctor
время . . . . time
Сколько времени? . . . . . . what time is it?
всё . . . . everything
вторник . . . . Tuesday
второй этаж . . . . second floor
вход . . . . entrance
входа нет . . . . do not enter
входить . . . . to enter
вчера . . . . yesterday
вы . . . . you
высокая . . . . high/tall
выход . . . . exit
выходить . . . . to go out, to exit

Г

газ . . . . natural gas
газета . . . . gazette, newspaper
газетчик . . . . newspaper man
галерея . . . . gallery
гараж . . . . garage
гастроном . . . delicatessen, grocery store
где . . . . where
география . . . . geography
геология . . . . geology
геолог . . . . geologist
геометрия . . . . geometry
гид . . . . guide
гимнастика . . . . gymnastics
гитара . . . . guitar
говорить . . . . to speak/say
говядина . . . . beef
год . . . . year
голоден . . . . hungry
горы . . . . mountains
горячая . . . . hot
гостиная . . . . living room
гостиница . . . . hotel/inn
градусы . . . . degrees
грамм . . . . gram
гранит . . . . granite
гребень . . . . comb
громко . . . . loudly
группа . . . . group
гусь . . . . goose

Д

да . . . . yes
дайте мне . . . . give me
дама . . . . dame, lady, woman
дата . . . . date
два, две . . . . two
двадцать . . . . twenty
двенадцать . . . . twelve
дверь . . . . door
девять . . . . nine
девятнадцать . . . . nineteen
девяносто . . . . ninety
дед . . . . grandfather

дезодоратор . . . . deodorant
декабре . . . . December
делать . . . . to do/make
   я делаю . . . . I do/make
делать пересадку . . . . to make a transfer
делегат . . . . delegate
день . . . . day
деньги . . . . money
десять . . . . ten
   десяти . . . . ten from
детей, дети . . . . children
дешёвая . . . . inexpemsive
джин . . . . gin
джаз . . . . jazz
диагноз . . . . diagnosis
диаграмма . . . . diagram, blueprint
диалоги . . . . dialogues/conversations
диван . . . . divan, couch
дизель . . . . diesel
диплом . . . . diploma
дипломат . . . . diplomat
директор . . . . director
дискуссия . . . . discussion
длинная . . . . long
для . . . . for
до . . . . until
доброе утро . . . . good morning
добрый вечер . . . . good evening
добрый день . . . . good day, good afternoon
до свидания . . . . goodbye
дождь . . . . raining
доктор . . . . doctor
документ . . . . document
доллар . . . . dollar
дом . . . . house
домашняя птица . . . . poultry
дорога . . . . road
дорогая . . . . expensive
дочь . . . . daughter
драма . . . . drama
друзья . . . . friends
душ . . . . shower
дядя . . . . uncle

Е

еврей . . . . Jewish man
еврейка . . . . Jewish woman
есть . . . . to eat
ехать . . . . to go

Ж

жакет . . . . woman's jacket
жареное . . . . roasted, fried
жарко . . . . hot
ждать . . . . to wait for
желе . . . . jelly
женщина . . . . woman
   женщины . . . . women
жёлтый . . . . yellow
жить . . . . to live/reside
журнал . . . . journal, magazine

З

за . . . . behind
завтра . . . . tomorrow
завтрак . . . . breakfast
заказывать . . . . to order/reserve
закрыто . . . . closed
занавес . . . . curtain
занята . . . . busy
запад . . . . west
   западный . . . . western
запеченное . . . . baked
звонок . . . . doorbell
здесь . . . . here
здоров . . . . healthy
зелёный . . . . green

зеркало . . . . mirror
зимой . . . . in winter
знать . . . . to know
зовут . . . . is called
   меня зовут . . . . . . I am called/my name is
зона . . . . zone
зонтик . . . . umbrella
зоопарк . . . . zoo
зубная паста . . . . toothpaste
зубная щётка . . . . toothbrush

И

и . . . . and
идти . . . . to go (on foot)
   я еду . . . . I go
   он/она идёт . . . . he/she goes
из . . . . out of/from
извините . . . . excuse me
изучать . . . . to learn
   я изучаю . . . . I learn
икра . . . . caviar
или . . . . or
имена . . . . names
импортный . . . . imported
имя . . . . name
Индия . . . . India
индустриальный . . . . industrial
инженер . . . . engineer
иностранный . . . . foreign
инспектор . . . . inspector
институт . . . . institute
инструктор . . . . instructor
инструкции . . . . instructions
инструмент . . . . instrument
интеллигент . . . . intellectual
интервью . . . . interview
интерес . . . . interest
интернациональный . . . . international
информация . . . . information
искать . . . . to look for
   я ищу . . . . I look for
Исландия . . . . Iceland
Ислания . . . . Spain
   по-испански . . . . in Spanish
история . . . . history
Италия . . . . Italy
   по-итальянски . . . . in Italian
июль . . . . July
июнь . . . . June

К

к себе . . . . pull (the doors)
кабина . . . . cabin, booth
кабинет . . . . study
каждые . . . . every
как . . . . how
   Как дела? . How are things?/How are you?
   какая, какие . . . . what kind of
какао . . . . cocoa
календарь . . . . calendar
камера . . . . camera
Канада . . . . Canada
канал . . . . canal
канарейка . . . . canary
кандидат . . . . candidate
канцтовары . . . . stationery store
капитал . . . . capital (money)
карандаш . . . . pencil
карта . . . . map
картина, картинка . . . . picture
касса . . . . ticket machine
кассир . . . . cashier
католик . . . . Catholic man
католичка . . . . Catholic woman
километр . . . . kilometer
кило . . . . kilo

кино . . . . cinema
киоск . . . . newsstand
класс . . . . class
   классик . . . . classic
клоун . . . . clown
книга . . . . book
книжный магазин . . . . bookstore
ковёр . . . . carpet
когда . . . . when
колбаса . . . . sausage
коллекция . . . . collection
комедия . . . . comedy
компас . . . . compass
композитор . . . . composer
коньяк . . . . cognac
конференция . . . . conference
комната . . . . room
конверт . . . . envelope
концерт . . . . concert
копеек копйки . . . . kopecks
корзина . . . . basket
коричневый . . . . brown
короткая . . . . short
кот . . . . cat
которая . . . . which
кофе . . . . coffee
краб . . . . crab
красивый . . . . pretty
красный . . . . red
Кремль . . . . Kremlin
кровать . . . . bed
кто . . . . who
Куба . . . . Cuba
купальный костюм . . . . swimsuit
купальный халат . . . . bathrobe
купить . . . . to buy
кухня . . . . kitchen

Л

лаборатория . . . . laboratory
лампа . . . . lamp
лево . . . . left
   налево . . . . to the left
Ленинград . . . . Leningrad
лет . . . . years
лететь . . . . to fly
   я лечу . . . . I fly
летом . . . . in summer
лимон . . . . lemon
лимонад . . . . lemonade
линия . . . . line
литература . . . . literature
литр . . . . liter
ложка . . . . spoon
любить . . . . to love
люди . . . . people

М

магазин . . . . store
май . . . . May
маленькая . . . . small
мало . . . . little
марка . . . . stamp
март . . . . March
масло . . . . butter
масса . . . . mass
мастер . . . . master
мать . . . . mother
математика . . . . mathematics
материя . . . . material
матрёшки . . . . Russian dolls
матч . . . . match (game)
машина . . . . machine (car)
   машина напрокат . . . . rental car
медаль . . . . medal
медь . . . . copper coins

медик . . . . medic
медицина . . . . medicine
медленно . . . . slow, slowly
между . . . . between
мелодия . . . . melody
мелочь . . . . change (coins)
меню . . . . menu
местный . . . . domestic, internal
месяцы . . . . months
металл . . . . metal
метод . . . . method
метро . . . . metro, subway
механик . . . . mechanic
микрофон . . . . microphone
милиция . . . . police
миллион . . . . million
миниатюра . . . . miniature
минут . . . . minutes
миссия . . . . mission
митинг . . . . meeting
много . . . . a lot, many
модель . . . . model
мой . . . . my
молодой . . . . young
молоко . . . . milk
молочная . . . . dairy
момент . . . . moment
монеты . . . . coins
Москва . . . . Moscow
мотор . . . . motor
мотоцикл . . . . motorcycle
мочь . . . . to be able to/can
мужчина . . . . man
мужчины . . . . men
музей . . . . museum
музыка . . . . music
мусульманин . . . . Moslem man
мусульманка . . . . Moslem woman
мы . . . . we
мыло . . . . soap
мясо . . . . meat
мяч . . . . ball

Н

на . . . . on, into
наверху . . . . upstairs
над . . . . over
название . . . . name
налево . . . . to the left
напишите . . . . write out
направо . . . . to the right
например . . . . for example
натуральный . . . . grilled
нация . . . . nation
начинается . . . . begins
не . . . . not, no
недел . . . . week
нейлон . . . . nylon
несерьёзный . . . . not serious
нет . . . . no
низкая . . . . low
никель . . . . nickel
новые . . . . new
нож . . . . knife
ноль . . . . zero
номер . . . . number
номере . . . . hotel room
норма . . . . norm, standard
нормальная . . . . normal
нос . . . . nose
носки . . . . socks
ночь . . . . night
ночная рубашка . . . . nightshirt
ноябрь . . . . November
нужно . . . . need
мне нужно . . . . I need
нужны . . . . necessary

О

обменять . . . . exchange
обед . . . . meal, dinner
овощи . . . . vegetables
овощной . . . . greengrocer's
одежда . . . . clothes
один . . . . one
одиннадцать . . . . eleven
одеяло . . . . blanket
окно . . . . window
октябрь . . . . October
оленина . . . . venison
олимпиада . . . . Olympics
он . . . . he
она . . . . she
они . . . . they
опаздывать . . . . to be late
оранжевый . . . . orange (color)
органист . . . . organist
опера . . . . opera
оркестр . . . . orchestra
оплатить . . . . to pay
опоздал . . . . late
осенью . . . . in autumn
остановка . . . . stop
остановка автобуса . . . . bus stop
остановка трамвая . . . . trolley stop
отварное . . . . boiled
ответы . . . . answers
отделение милиции . . . . police station
отделы . . . . shops, departments
отель . . . . hotel
отец . . . . father
открытка . . . . postcard
открыто . . . . open
отправление . . . . departure
от себя . . . . push (the doors)
отходить . . . to depart (trains, buses, ships)
офицер . . . . officer
официальный . . . . official
официант . . . . waiter
официантка . . . . waitress
очень . . . . very
очки . . . . eyeglasses

П

павильон . . . . pavilion
пакет . . . . package
пальто . . . . overcoat
пансионат . . . . . pension, boarding house
парад . . . . parade
парикмахерская . . . . hairdresser
парк . . . . park
парламент . . . . parliament
партия . . . . party
паспорт . . . . passport
пассажир . . . . passenger
перед . . . . in front of
перо . . . . pen
перчатки . . . . gloves
перец . . . . pepper
пианист . . . . pianist
пиво . . . . beer
пижама . . . . pajamas
пикник . . . . picnic
пилот . . . . pilot
писать . . . . to write
письмо . . . . letter
пить . . . . to drink
платформа . . . . platform
плащ . . . . raincoat
плита . . . . stove
плохо . . . . bad
пляж . . . . beach
по . . . . on
повторять . . . . to repeat

Р

под . . . . under
подвал . . . . basement
подушка . . . . pillow
поезд . . . . train
поездка . . . . trip
пожар . . . . fire
позвонить . . . . . . to telephone/call
позиция . . . . position
погода . . . . weather
пожалуйста . . . . . . please/you're welcome
полиция . . . . police
половина . . . . half
полотенца . . . . towels
показывать . . . . to show
покупать . . . . to buy
понедельник . . . . Monday
понимать . . . . to understand
порт . . . . port
портрет . . . . portrait
посылать . . . . to send
посылка . . . . package
потолок . . . . ceiling
потом . . . . then
почему . . . . why
почта . . . . mail, post office
почтовое отделение . . . . post office
почтовый ящик . . . . mailbox
поэт . . . . poet
правильно . . . . correct
править . . . . to drive
право . . . . right
направо . . . . to the right
православная . . . . Orthodox woman
православный . . . . Orthodox man
практика . . . . practice
прачечная . . . . laundry
приезд . . . . arrival
приезжать . . . . to arrive
примеры . . . . examples
приходить . . to arrive (trains, buses, ships)
программа . . . . program
прогресс . . . . progress
продавать . . . . to sell
продмаг . . . . food store
продукт . . . . product
проект . . . . project
профессия . . . . profession
профессор . . . . professor
процент . . . . percent
прямо . . . . straight ahead
пряники . . . . pastries
путешественник . . . . traveler
путешествовать . . . . to travel
пятнадцать . . . . fifteen
пять . . . . five
пятьдесят . . . . fifty
пятьсот . . . . five hundred
пятница . . . . Friday

Р

радио . . . . radio
разговор по телефону . . . . telephone
conversation
размер . . . . size
Который размер? . . . . Which size?
ракета . . . . rocket
ранг . . . . rank
рапорт . . . . report
расписание . . . . schedule
револьвер . . . . revolver
революция . . . . revolution
регистрация . . . . registration
резервация . . . . reservation
рекорд . . . . record
религия . . . . religion
ресторан . . . . restaurant
родители . . . . parents
родственники . . . . relatives
розовый . . . . pink
рубль/рубли . . . . ruble/rubles

русский . . . . Russian
по-русски . . . . in Russian
русские . . . . Russians
ручка . . . . pen
рыбный рынок . . . . fish market
рыба . . . . fish
рынок . . . . market
рядом с . . . . next to

С

с . . . . with
сад . . . . garden
салат . . . . salad
салфетка . . . . napkin
самовар . . . . samovar
самолёт . . . . airplane
сандалии . . . . sandals
сапоги . . . . boots
свинина . . . . pork
сдача . . . . change
север . . . . north
северный . . . . northern
сегодня . . . . today
сезон . . . . season
секретарь . . . . secretary
секунда . . . . second
семинар . . . . seminar
семнадцать . . . . seventeen
семь . . . . seven
семьдесят . . . . seventy
семья . . . . family
сентябрь . . . . September
серебро . . . . silver coins
серый . . . . gray
сестра . . . . sister
сигара . . . . cigar
сигарета . . . . cigarette
симфония . . . . symphony
синий . . . . blue
сколько . . . . how much
Сколько времени? . . . . . . What time is it?
словарь . . . . dictionary
слово . . . . word
слон . . . . elephant
снег . . . . snow
собака . . . . dog
советский . . . . Soviet
Советский Союз . . . . Soviet Union
соль . . . . salt
сорок . . . . forty
спальня . . . . bedroom
спасибо . . . . thank you
спать . . . . to sleep
спокойной ночи . . . . good night
спросить . . . . to ask
я спрашиваю . . . . I ask
среда . . . . Wednesday
ставить . . . . park/put
стадион . . . . stadium
стакан . . . . glass
станция . . . . station
станция метро . . . . metro station
старый . . . . old
старейший . . . . oldest
старт . . . . start
стена . . . . wall
стирать . . . . to wash/clean (clothes)
сто . . . . one hundred
стоит . . . . costs
стол . . . . table
столовая . . . . dining room
стоянка . . . . parking lot, taxi stand
страница . . . . page
стригут . . . . (they) cut
студент . . . . student
стул . . . . chair
суббота . . . . Saturday
сувениры . . . . souvenirs
сумка . . . . purse/bag
суп . . . . soup

Счастливого пути! . . . . . Have a good trip!
счёт . . . . bill
сын . . . . son

Т

табак . . . . tobacco
такси . . . . taxi
там . . . . there (is)
тарелка . . . . plate
театр . . . . theater
телевизор . . . . television
телеграмма . . . . telegram
телескоп . . . . telescope
телефон . . . . telephone
телефон-автомат . . . . . . public telephone
телятина . . . . veal
температура . . . . temperature
теперь . . . . now
терять . . . . to lose
тётя . . . . aunt
тихо . . . . softly
тогда . . . . then
тоже . . . . also
толстая . . . . thick
только . . . . only
томат . . . . tomato
тонкая . . . . thin
тост . . . . toast
трамвай . . . . street car/trolley
три . . . . three
тридцать . . . . thirty
тринадцать . . . . thirteen
триста . . . . three hundred
трубка . . . . receiver (telephone)
туалет . . . . toilet
туман . . . . fog
турист . . . . tourist
туфли . . . . shoes
тушёное . . . . stewed
тысяча . . . . one thousand

У

у вас есть . . . . you have
у меня есть . . . . I have
у нас есть . . . . we have
уезжать . . . . to leave
я уезжаю . . . . I leave
угол . . . . corner
удачи . . . . good luck
указания . . . . directions
укладывать . . . . to pack
я укладываю . . . . I pack
улица . . . . street
умывальник . . . . washstand
универмаг . . . . department store
универсальный магазин . department store
университет . . . . university
утро . . . . morning

Ф

Фаренгейт . . . . Fahrenheit
фаршированый . . . . stuffed
февраль . . . . February
фильм . . . . film
фотоаппарат . . . . camera
фотограф . . . . photographer
фотомагазин . . . . camera store
фотоплёнка . . . . film
Франция . . . . France
по-французски . . . . in French
фрукт . . . . fruit
футбол . . . . soccer, football

Х

химически . . . . chemically
химчистка . . . . dry cleaner's
хлеб . . . . bread

холодильник . . . . refrigerator
холодная . . . . cold
хорошо . . . . good
не хорошо . . . . not good
хорошо сидит . . . . it fits well
хочу . . . . (I) would like
я хочу пить . . . . I have thirst

Ц

царь . . . . czar, tsar
цвет . . . . color
цветок . . . . flower
Цельсий . . . . Celsius
центр . . . . city center
церковь . . . . church
цирк . . . . circus

Ч

чай . . . . tea
час . . . . o'clock/hour
Который час? . . . . What time is it?
часто . . . . often
часы . . . . clock, watch
чашка . . . . cup
чемодан . . . . suitcase
четверть . . . . a quarter (toward)
четверг . . . . Thursday
четыре . . . . four
четырнадцать . . . . fourteen
чёрный . . . . black
числа . . . . numbers
чистый . . . . clean
читать . . . . to read
я читаю . . . . I read
что . . . . what
чулки . . . . stockings

Ш

шарф . . . . scarf
Швеция . . . . Sweden
по-шведски . . . . in Swedish
шестнадцать . . . . sixteen
шесть . . . . six
шестьдесят . . . . sixty
шкаф . . . . wardrobe/cupboard
школа . . . . school
шляпа . . . . hat
шоссе . . . . main road
штат . . . . state
шторм . . . . storm
шьёт . . . . sews

Э

экватор . . . . equator
экзамен . . . . exam
экономика . . . . economics
экспресс . . . . express
эра . . . . era
эскалатор . . . . escalator
этаж . . . . floor (of building)
это/этой/эти/этот . . . . that/this
Это всё . . . . That's all.

Ю

юг . . . . south
южный . . . . southern

Я

я I
яблоко . . . . apple
язык . . . . language, tongue
январь . . . . January
янтарь . . . . amber
Япония . . . . Japan
яхта . . . . yacht

DRINKING GUIDE

This guide is intended to explain the variety of beverages available to you while in the Soviet Union. It is by no means complete. Some of the experimenting has been left up to you, but this should get you started. One asterisk indicates a brand name, while two asterisks indicate a regional variety.

ГОРЯЧИЕ НАПИТКИ (hot drinks)

чай с лимоном	tea with lemon
чай с вареньем	tea with jam
чай с молоком	tea with milk
чай с мёдом	tea with honey

Чай was traditionally made in a samovar, **самовар.** A very strong tea was made in a teapot, which was kept warm on top of the samovar. A small portion of the tea was poured into a cup and diluted with hot water from the samovar.

кофе	coffee
кофе с молоком	coffee with milk
чёрный кофе	black coffee
кофе по-восточному	Turkish coffee
кофе-гляссе	coffee with ice cream
какао	cocoa

ХОЛОДНЫЕ НАПИТКИ (cold drinks)

молоко	milk
фруктовый коктейль	milkshake
кефир	sour milk (usually topped with sugar)
ряженка	thick, sour milk
кисель	sour-fruit drink
лимонад	lemonade
байкал	cola drink
* пепси-кола	Pepsi-Cola
квас	kvass

Квас is a dark, non-alcoholic beverage made from yeast and black bread. Although it is not sold in restaurants, it is readily available from street vendors.

минеральная вода	mineral water
* Нарзан	
* Ессентуки	
* Боржоми	

You'll find that most mineral waters in Russia are domestic, bottled from natural spring-water from the Caucasus.

фруктовый сок	fruit juice
апельсиновый сок	orange juice
яблочный сок	apple juice
виноградный сок	grape juice
кнюквенный морс	cranberry juice
сливовый сок	prune juice
абрикосовый сок	apricot juice
гранатовый сок	pomegranate juice
персиковый сок	peach juice
томатный сок	tomato juice

Don't miss a chance to sample Russian fruit juices. They are delicious. You'll find juice bars in the larger grocery stores.

ПИВО (beer)

светлое пиво	light beer
тёмное пиво	dark beer
* Московское	
* Ленинградское	
* Двойное золотое	
* Рижское	

Пиво is available in restaurants, but if you're visiting the Soviet Union during the summer, you'll want to visit the streetside beer stalls.

СПИРТНЫЕ НАПИТКИ (alcohol)

Both **спиртные напитки** and **вино** can be purchased by the bottle or by weight. A shot is 50 grams and a glass of wine is approximately 150 grams.

водка	vodka
* Экстра	
* Столичная	
* Русская	
* Пшеничная	
* Смирновская	
* Охотничья	
Коньяк	cognac
**Армянский коньяк	Armenian cognac
**Грузинский коньяк	Georgian cognac
виски	whiskey
джин	gin
ром	rum
аперитив	aperitif
ликёр	liqueur

ВИНО (wine)

красное вино	red wine
**Алазанская долина	Georgian wine
**Мукузани	Georgian wine
булое вино	white wine
**Цинандали	Georgian wine
розовое вино	rosé wine
вермут	vermouth
портвейн	port
херес	sherry
шампанское	champagne
сухое шампанское	dry champagne
полу-сухое шампанское	semi-dry champagne
сладкое шампанское	sweet champagne
полу-сладкое шампанское	semi-sweet champagne
* Игристое	
* Золотое	

Russian champagne and **вино** from Georgia, a region in Caucasia, are considered to be some of the finest wines in the world. They are rated for their quality on a star system: seven stars indicates a superlative wine, while one star indicates a wine of lesser quality.

Меню
menu

FOLD HERE

FOLD HERE

Завтрак? Обед? Или Ужин?

отварное	boiled
жареное	roasted
тушёное	stewed
запеченное	baked
фаршированный	stuffed
на вертеле	grilled on a skewer
в сметане	in a sour cream sauce
в томате	in a tomato sauce
паровой	steamed
мало прожаренный	rare
не сильно прожаренный	medium
хорошо прожаренный	well-done

Что мне нужно? (what do I need?)

масло	butter
сахар	sugar
варенье	jam
мёд	honey
соль	salt
перец	pepper
уксус	vinegar
растительное масло	oil
оливкое масло	olive oil
горчица	mustard
соус	sauce, gravy
сыр	cheese
вода	water
лед	ice
майонез	mayonnaise
сливки	cream
сметана	sour cream
кефир	sour milk
творог	cottage cheese

Птица и Дичь (poultry and game)

курица/цыплята	chicken
гусь	goose
утка	duck
индейка	turkey
рябчик	hazel grouse
тетерев	black grouse
куропатка	partridge
вальдшнеп	woodcock
бекас	snipe
чирок	teal
перепел	quail
кролик	rabbit
оленина	venison
цыплята жареные	fried chicken
куриные крокеты	chicken croquettes
белое мясо курицы	breast of chicken
котлеты по-киевски	chicken Kiev

Овощи (vegetables)

баклажаны	eggplant
горох	peas
грибы	mushrooms
капуста	cabbage
красная капуста	red cabbage
цветная капуста	cauliflower
картофель	potatoes
картофель жареный	fried potatoes
картофель отварной	boiled potatoes
картофель пюре	mashed potatoes
картофель в сметане	potatoes in sour cream
кукуруза	corn
лук	onions
морковь	carrots
перец	pepper/green pepper
перец горький	pimentos
петрушка	parsley
помидоры	tomatoes
редиска	radishes
репа	turnips
свекла	beets
шпинат	spinach

(pree-yaht-nah-vah) (ahp-peh-tee-tah)
Приятного аппетита!

Салат (salad)

салат из белых грибов	white-mushroom salad
салат из столичный	meat-and-vegetable salad
винегрет	vinaigrette of vegetables
соус винегрет	vinaigrette
соус фруктово-ягодный	berry, fruit sauce

Десерт (dessert)

мороженое	ice cream
ванильное мороженое	vanilla ice cream
шоколадное мороженое	chocolate ice cream
кисель	jello-style dessert
компот	compote
крем	whipped cream
пудинг	pudding
рисовый пудинг	rice pudding
лимон с сахаром	lemon with sugar
яблоки в вине	apples in wine
шоколадный соус	chocolate sauce
торт	torte, cake
кекс	muffin
пирог	pie
пряники	cookies
пирожные	pastries, small cakes
печенье	pastries, biscuits
коржики	shortcakes

Фрукты (fruit)

апельсин	orange
арбуз	watermelon
банан	banana
виноград	grapes
вишни	cherries
грейпфрут	grapefruit
груша	pear
дыня	melon
земляника	strawberries
дыня	cantaloupe
лимон	lemon
малина	raspberries
персик	peach
чёрная смородина	blackberries
яблоко	apple
ягоды	berries

Закуски (appetizers)

икра	caviar
икра грибная	mushroom caviar
красная икра	red caviar
чёрная икра	black caviar
сардины	sardines
сельдь	herring
креветки	shrimp
балык	smoked sturgeon
сосиски	sausages
колбаса	cold cuts
копчёная колбаса	smoked cold cuts
паштет	pâté
студень	aspic
форшмак	potato-and-meat hash
бутерброды открытые	open-faced sandwiches
бутерброды закрытые	sandwiches

Хлеб (bread and dough dishes)

чёрный хлеб	black bread
белый хлеб	white bread
ржаной хлеб	rye bread
пшеничный хлеб	wheat bread
булочки	rolls
блины	pancakes
блины с маслом и сметаной	pancakes with butter and sour cream
пельмени	small dumplings
каша	buckwheat, cereal
манная	farina
пирожки	baked, stuffed dumplings
кулебяка	breaded fish loaf
рис	rice
макароны	macaroni
пирог с грибами	mushroom pie
пирог с капустой	cabbage pie
пирог с луком	onion pie
пирог с мясом	meat pie

Яйца (eggs)

яйца вкрутую	hard-boiled eggs
яйца всмятку	soft-boiled eggs
яичница	fried eggs
взбитая яичница	scrambled eggs
фаршированные яйца	stuffed eggs
яйца с икрой	eggs with caviar

FOLD HERE

Суп (soup)

борщ	borsch
борщ со свининой	borsch with pork
щи	cabbage soup
щи суточные	sauerkraut soup
уха	fish soup
лапша	noodle soup
молочная лапша	milk soup with noodles
суп-грибной	mushroom soup
суп-овощной	vegetable soup
суп-пюре из овощей	vegetable purée
суп молочный с овощами	cream-of-vegetable soup
суп из фасоли	bean soup
суп картофельный	potato soup
суп гороховый	pea soup
солянка	spicy, thick soup
рисовый суп	rice soup
бульон	bouillon
бульон с яйцом	bouillon with an egg
бульон с фрикадельками	bouillon with meatballs
рассольник	kidney-and-cucumber soup

Рыба (fish dishes)

треска	cod
камбала	flounder
карп	carp
лосось	salmon
кета	Siberian salmon
щука	pike
раки	crayfish
краб	crab
окунь	perch
судак	pike perch
палтус	halibut
форель	trout
осетрина	sturgeon
осетрина в томате	sturgeon in tomato sauce
осетрина под маринадом	pickled sturgeon
севрюга	type of sturgeon
осетрина „фри"	fried sturgeon
судак „фри"	fried pike perch

Мясо (meat dishes)

баранина	mutton
ветчина	ham
говядина	beef
свинина	pork
телятина	veal

FOLD HERE

Мясо (meat dishes)

бараньи котлеты	lamb chops
ветчина жареная	fried ham
колбаса жареная	fried sausages
мозги жареные	fried brains
телятина жареная	roast veal
мясо жареное в сметане	meat roasted in sour cream and onions
с луком	cream and onions
ростбиф	roast beef
поджарка	roast pork
бефстроганов	beef Stroganoff
бифштекс	beefsteak
рагу	stew
говядина тушеная	beef stew
говядина в сухарях	breaded beef
рулет	meatloaf
гуляш	goulash
котлеты	chopped beef
шашлык	shashlik, kebabs
долма	stuffed grape leaves
голубцы	stuffed cabbage
мясные котлеты	
котлеты свиные отбивные	breaded pork chops
отбивные из баранины	breaded lamb chops
котлеты натуральные из баранины	grilled lamb chops
шницель	breaded veal cutlet
язык	tongue
печёнка	liver
сосиски	sausages
сардельки	small sausages
бекон	bacon
битки/биточки	meatballs
почки	kidneys
купаты	spicy pork sausage
плов	pilaf

Салат (salad)

салат из фруктов	fruit salad
салат из огурцов	cucumber salad
салат из помидоров	tomato salad
салат из фасоли	bean salad
салат из редиса	radishes with sour cream
салат картофельный	potato salad
салат из капусты с яблоками	cabbage-and-apple salad

(yah) *(zah-kah-zih-vah-yoo)* **я заказываю**	*(yah)* *(yeh-doo)* **я еду**
(yah) *(pah-koo-pah-yoo)* **я покупаю**	*(yah)* *(pree-yez-zhy-yoo)* **я приезжаю**
(yah) *(ee-zoo-chah-yoo)* **я изучаю**	*(yah)* *(vee-zhoo)* **я вижу**
(yah) *(pohv-tar-yah-yoo)* **я повторяю**	*(yah)* *(zhee-voo)* **я живу**
(yah) *(poh-nee-mah-yoo)* **я понимаю**	*(yah)* *(zhdoo)* **я жду**
(yah) *(gah-vah-ryoo)* **я говорю**	*(yah)* *(eesh-choo)* **я ищу**

I go	I order/reserve
I arrive/come	I buy
I see	I learn
I live	I repeat
I wait for	I understand
I look for	I speak/say

(yah) *(yem)* **Я ЕМ**	*(yah)* *(prah-dah-yoo)* **Я ПРОДАЮ**
(yah) *(pyoo)* **Я ПЬЮ**	*(yah)* *(pah-sih-lah-yoo)* **Я ПОСЫЛАЮ**
(yah) *(hah-choo)* **Я ХОЧУ**	*(yah)* *(splyoo)* **Я СПЛЮ**
(men-yeh) *(noozh-nah)* **МНЕ НУЖНО**	*(yah)* *(zvah-nyoo)* **Я ЗВОНЮ**
(men-yah) *(zah-voot)* **МЕНЯ ЗОВУТ…**	*(die-tee)* *(men-yeh)* **ДАЙТЕ МНЕ**
(oo) *(men-yah)* *(yest)* **У МЕНЯ ЕСТЬ**	*(yah)* *(pee-shoo)* **Я ПИШУ**

I sell	I eat
I send	I drink
I sleep	I would like
I phone	I need
give me...	my name is...
I write	I have

(yah) *(pah-kah-zih-vah-yoo)*	*(yah)* *(lee-choo)*
Я ПОКАЗЫВАЮ	**Я ЛЕЧУ**

(yah) *(plah-choo)* *(zah)*	*(yah)* *(prahv-lyoo)*
Я ПЛАЧУ ЗА	**Я ПРАВЛЮ**

(yah) *(znah-yoo)*	*(yah)* *(oo-yez-zhah-yoo)*
Я ЗНАЮ	**Я УЕЗЖАЮ**

(yah) *(mah-goo)*	*(yah)* *(dyeh-lah-yoo)*
Я МОГУ	**Я ДЕЛАЮ**

(yah) *(chee-tah-yoo)*	*(yah)* *(dyeh-lah-yoo)* *(pyair-yeh-sahd-koo)*
Я ЧИТАЮ	**Я ДЕЛАЮ ПЕРЕСАДКУ**

(yah) *(poot-yeh-shest-voo-yoo)*	*(yah)* *(oo-klah-dih-vah-yoo)*
Я ПУТЕШЕСТВУЮ	**Я УКЛАДЫВАЮ**

I fly	I show
I drive	I pay for
I leave	I know
I do/make	I can
I make a transfer	I read
I pack	I travel

(poh-yezd) *(ah-pahz-dih-vah-yet)*	*(yah)* *(zah-krih-vah-yoo)*
Поезд опаздывает.	**я закрываю**

(poh-yezd) *(pree-hah-deet)* *(vuh)*	*(yah)* *(aht-krih-vah-yoo)*
Поезд приходит в…	**я открываю**

(poh-yezd) *(aht-hoh-deet)* *(vuh)*	*(yah)* *(koor-yoo)*
Поезд отходит в…	**я курю**

(yah) *(stee-rah-yoo)*	*(yah)* *(lyoob-lyoo)*
я стираю	**я люблю**

(yah) *(tyair-yah-yoo)*	*(yah)* *(sprah-shee-vah-yoo)*
я теряю	**я спрашиваю**

(yah) *(rah-boh-tah-yoo)*	*(yah)* *(nah-chee-nah-yoo)*
я работаю	**я начинаю**

I close	The train is late.
I open	The train arrives at...
I smoke	The train departs at...
I like	I wash
I ask	I lose
I begin	I work

(zah-nee-mah-yet) **занимает**	*(eez-vee-nee-tee)* **извините**
(skohl-kah) *(et-tah)* *(stoy-eet)* **Сколько это стоит?**	*(ee-dyoht)* *. (dohzhd)* **Идёт дождь.**
(kahk) *(dee-lah)* **Как дела?**	*(ee-dyoht)* *(snyeg)* **Идёт снег.**
(doh) *(svee-dahn-yah)* **До свиданья!**	*(see-vohd-nyah)* **сегодня**
(pah-zhahl-yes-tah) **пожалуйста**	*(zahv-trah)* **завтра**
(spah-see-bah) **спасибо**	*(vchee-rah)* **вчера**

excuse me	it takes
It is raining.	How much does this cost?
It is snowing.	How are things/ How are you?
today	good bye!
tomorrow	please/you're welcome
yesterday	thank-you

(zdah-rohv) *(bohl-yen)* **здоров - болен**	*(tohl-stah-yah)* *(tohn-kah-yah)* **толстая - тонкая**
(hah-rah-shoh) *(ploh-hah)* **хорошо - плохо**	*(nahd)* *(pohd)* **над - под**
(gor-yah-chah-yah) *(hah-lohd-nah-yah)* **горячая - холодная**	*(lyev-ah)* *(prah-vah)* **лево - право**
(tee-hah) *(grohm-kah)* **тихо - громко**	*(myed-lyen-nah)* *(bis-trah)* **медленно - быстро**
(kah-roht-kah-yah) *(dleen-nah-yah)* **короткая - длинная**	*(vwee-soh-kah-yah)* *(nees-kah-yah)* **высокая - низкая**
(vwee-soh-kah-yah) *(mah-lyen-kah-yah)* **высокая - маленькая**	*(stah-ree)* *(mah-lah-doy)* **старый - молодой**

thick - thin	healthy - sick
above - below	good - bad
left - right	hot - cold
slow - fast	softly - loudly
high - low	short - long
old - young	tall/high - small

(doh-rah-gah-yah) *(dyeh-shyoh-vah-yah)* **дорогая - дешёвая**	*(yah)* **я**
(boh-gaht) *(byed-yen)* **богат - беден**	*(ohn)* **он**
(mnoh-gah) *(mah-lah)* **много - мало**	*(oh-nah)* **она**
(aht-krit-tah) *(zah-krit-tah)* **открыто - закрыто**	*(mwee)* **мы**
(slahd-kee) *(kees-lee)* **сладкий - кислый**	*(vwee)* **вы**
(bohl-shoy) *(mah-lyen-kee)* **большой - маленький**	*(oh-nee)* **они**

I	expensive-inexpensive
he	rich - poor
she	a lot - a little
we	open - closed
you	sweet - sour
they	big - small